Economic Ecology

Baselines for Urban Development

Economic Ecology

Baselines for Urban Development

By
JAMES L. GREEN

. . . . .

. . .

.

UNIVERSITY OF GEORGIA PRESS - ATHENS

In Memory of

CHARLES O. EMMERICH

Contents

Foreword

OFTEN in times of crisis, when men are seeking answers to serious problems, a man appears who can lead the way.

Charles O. Emmerich, to whom this book is dedicated, was such a man. He recognized that response to the accelerating pace of urban change was a matter of personal and urban citizen philosophy as well as direct determination of human values, motivations, and specific urban programs. The author of this discourse and I gained valuable insights and much understanding of urban people and urban problems through our association with C. O. Emmerich. He understood the requirements a demanding public places upon public and business leaders when the urban environment fails to meet adequately the needs of the people. His contributions as a public leader will stand the test of time.

Professor Green's ecological approach to economic-social-political urban development uses an idea of system to unify our knowledge of human relationships and behavior. His ultimate conception of a *market* system as the protector of individual liberty, the controller of economic affairs, and the institutional framework through which an urban society can satisfy its demands is a useful abstraction. The whole idea gives the reader the feeling that the social scientists who study urban problems are getting down to the basic meanings and needs of an urban system development. Green's approach provides an extension and broadening of perspective, a deeper understanding based on human ecological development.

The abstraction developed here is an idea. Ideas may be value-less or invaluable because much depends upon how we use them. The ideas developed in this ecological setting give the reader a real sense of personal interconnection with the past and with the dynamic and moving urban world of today.

Of real significance is the fact that Professor Green's ideas and assumptions are not solely the product of a detached academic, but combine his activist role as a consultant and adviser at the grass roots level of urban affairs.

All urban citizens who seek a fuller understanding of the homeostatic forces influencing the totality of the environment in which they work and live should read this book.

DAN SWEAT
Director of Governmental Liaison
City of Atlanta

Preface

THERE is scarcely any person or agency or institution that is not critically involved with the major socio-political-economic problems of our times. Economic ecology, in the writer's view, is as broad-gauged and universal as public health, the quality of education, the conservation of natural resources, the beauty of our forests and our cities, and the non-technical exploits of our space program. In all these things society is inherently interested and involved. Economic ecology provides a multifaceted approach to problems that confront us all as human beings, for economic ecology is human ecology. Men have the means to control their environment and to design the economic games they wish to play.

A study of economic ecology offers social scientists and community leaders in government, business, and all related agencies a basis for choice. If we are, in fact, on the crest of a fundamental rethinking of the divisions of public and private sector activity and social involvement, the current ecological moment of change may have major significance. This study of economic ecology linking the various forces in human economic affairs examines in its final stages the deepening crises of our time as they relate to the changing complexities of our dynamic urban environment.

In the essence of Western tradition society's *business* has been *business*. Men who directed behavior of other men in production processes and determined the distribution of income from production ascended to leadership positions in the community. From his early civilized beginnings man in the Western world has concerned himself with liberty, freedom of choice, and abundance. In economic ecological change can be seen the "system" developments that demonstrate man's rationality and intellectual genius. An understanding of past ecological system movements can assist man in the choices he currently faces.

The base on which economic ecology must rest is set forth in the first chapter. In their quest to organize themselves and natural resources in response to economic needs, men began by institutionalizing economic relationships. Concomitantly, as some men set forth rules governing the behavior of all men, value issues arose. In the Protestant ethic, for example, the standard that every man must work by the sweat of his brow permeates Western culture and economic "system" ecology. The necessity of work and concepts of freedom of choice and abundance infiltrate the theme of this study as urgent value issues of our times—note specifically, the minimum income proposal. As man moved through history his tools improved, his productivity was enhanced, and his innate tendency to "barter and truck" led gradually to development of the market system.

The prime problems of production and distribution are outlined and placed within the framework of early market capitalism. As integral facets of market functioning, the market oriented parameters of individualism, rationality, and market automaticity are introduced. These are human forces influencing the price mechanism and the market organization of economic affairs. In the Western world the market determined the economic environment. Ecological change now is reflected in changes in market behavior, market structure, and market functioning.

Ecological modification of the market system evolves through man's organizational genius. We seek in this analysis to provide an understanding of market system dynamics. The move from the simplistic theology of classical economics to the highly oligopolistic and organized market structure of today's urban business community points to a reversal in the exercise of economic power. This ecological movement brings the reader to the brink of urban crises. Business has created a potent production economy; should the private corporation respond to the ecological challenges by adapting to dynamic changes in the social and economic characteristics of urban environments? Is there a system change in the offing, particularly with new non-economic challenges and social responsibilities calling insistently for attention?

If economic ecology is indeed human ecology then the individual quest for liberty, freedom of choice, and abundance is of great significance to us. This in our frame of reference is looked upon as the human quest for economic citizenship. Development of the market system brought forth a new set of rules governing economic behavior. Citizenship with its connotations of dignity, belonging, freedom of choice and action was won by group after group, but the price was high. In this instance, past human relationships lend much credence to full understanding of present socio-economic movements. In fact, current articulations of dissatisfaction with the "system" are not new phenomena, but rather reflect a vibrant and viable democracy at work. Indeed, at this moment in time enlightened citizens realize the need for an intellectual revitalization to ease and smooth the ecological adaptation to the urban environment we have created.

This work is designed to build the foundation and the processes for understanding and meeting today's urban development needs. The processes and complexities of growth and stabilization requirements are illustrated in terms of economic flow, productivity, employment, and income. These basic economic relationships and processes encompass those forces and system principles which create or fail to create urban economic viability. Urban economic health, in turn, penetrates into every niche and corner of the urban community; no person or firm can afford to ignore or fail to understand basic economic development processes in today's specialized, inter-dependent, monetized urban market economy.

This book is directed to students of urban affairs and intelligent citizens whose political-social-economic-cultural relationships are by-product determinants of urban environments. Value judgments are not avoided in this inter-disciplinary analysis. The primary tool used is not statistics, but rather scholarly specialization and thought. This work reflects a strong commitment to enterprising democratic processes as exemplified in modern urban developments.

ACKNOWLEDGEMENTS

No thesis is developed in a vacuum. Former teachers, associates, and a wide selection of structured and non-structured readings and experiences contribute in ways not always recognized. The ideas expressed in this book came from many sources, though any error is mine. Those who have tried to save me from error in giving of their time, talent, and counsel receive my sincere thanks.

Among those who have helped specifically are: Professor George Horton of Auburn University, Professors Jerry Padgett, William Shenkel, Anthony Nemetz, and Earnest Melvin of the University of Georgia. Dr. Chong Soo Pyun of the Federal Reserve Bank of Atlanta assisted significantly. My sincere thanks to James Reid for the tedious task of verification of sources of quoted data.

Misses Noel Curth and Patsy Chastain, and Mrs. Nancy Myrich are due my sincere gratitude for typing and proofing the manuscript.

College of Business Administration   JAMES L. GREEN
University of Georgia

.. 1 ..

Infrastructure of Economic Reality

ECONOMIC ecology is *not* the study of economic history as a narration of past economic relationships nor is it a review or a compilation of the history of economic thought. Economic ecology *is* the study of man's adaptation to and creation of an economic environment resulting from those forces that maintain a dynamic society. Economic ecology is institutional and "system oriented," reflecting man's organizational and innovative abilities. Economic ecology, then, illuminates economic movement and provides an insight into human behavior and relationships including the social, the economic, the political, and the cultural forces which motivate man and structure his environment.

Man is, and has always been, a versatile problem solver. He is an organizer—a thinking, feeling, rational, and acquisitive being. As an economic being, *Man is as he thinks and does.* Consequently, human society tends to be institutional and system oriented in its basic foundation and structure. Using his intellectual rationality, man has devised "system" relationships which organize, direct, and control the patterns of human behavior. Through the ages, men have accepted law and custom as the basis for social and economic order. In so many ways, men's actions follow a set plan of ordering, operating, and proceeding. This study of economic ecology places emphasis on the man-made economic environment as it is imposed upon and interacts with the natural environment. In the framework of economic ecology, man's pragmatic adjustments to an essentially antagonistic natural environment reflect a continuing ferment in institutional arrangements. As men in their adaptive and creative behavior change the rules governing play of the economic game, they implicitly change the game itself. Through institutional and "system" modification man adapts to

1

changing environmental requirements. The system of political economy devised by man and the institutional structure within which the system operates revolves around the intricacies stemming from the two primary problems facing man as he interacts with nature: (1) the production of goods and services, and (2) the distribution of the "fruits" of production.

ECOLOGICAL ADAPTATION TO SCARCITY

Economically, the fact and reality of relative scarcity has caused man's dilemma and, at the same time, his most prominent intellectual challenge. Man's origins as an organized economic and social being are lost in the dimness of the past. He has, however, moved through time making continuous adaptations to his changing environment. Always, the theme of relative scarcity has dominated economic doctrine and economic reality.

Adaptation to an antagonistic natural environment with relatively scarce productive resources required an intellectual organization of human and physical resources which would deliver the greatest output of goods and services relative to the input of scarce productive factors. Solutions to the production problem in these terms are essentially "system" solutions. Under varying environmental conditions diverse system arrangements are needed to motivate and control human behavior in economic activities. In every instance the intellectual intent has been to obtain that "mix" of productive factors that would optimize the allocation and utilization of scarce resources. In this ecological context, the various systems and institutional arrangements devised in the man-made economic environment provided answers to the universal economic questions: What to produce, how much to produce, and how to produce, i.e., what "mix" of productive factors to use.

The co-equal problem challenging man's intellectual rationality was (and is) to devise system arrangements that optimize the distribution of income from production. The system and its institutional arrangements must somehow distribute income so as to accommodate the system itself and protect the integrity of its functioning. The system must order economic affairs so as to motivate and direct human behavior, and as a consequence must encompass those who contribute directly to the production process and those who, although they contribute no "sweat from their brows" directly in production, do nonetheless claim a share of the income created.

"System" Extends beyond the Economic

The requirement that the system "direct" men as well as motivate them introduces both the stick and the carrot. Society constitutes a community of intermingling, interdependent individuals. In this community, society, through its devised system of rules, both implicit and explicit, directs the conduct, standards, and activities of its members. In this sense, every social organization is cemented into a viable unit through voluntary individual actions coordinated by the established rules of the game and by coercion. In the sense of its use here, coercion need not necessarily imply force or control stemming from hierarchical economic status, military, or some related institutional arrangement giving one person a "command" position over another. Coercion governing individual behavioral patterns also stems from social habit, tradition, and custom. These are powerful forces in human society, and social ostracism constitutes a potent weapon of social control. Change of the standards of the society is a slow and oftentimes troublesome process and seems to provide substance for the perennial "generation gap" that separates father and son.

In the western tradition of economic liberalism and democratic political institutions, individual freedom of action has long been a cherished social and economic value. Coercion of the individual is inherent in society, yet the evolving "system" of enterprising capitalism is one based essentially on voluntary cooperation and mutual interdependencies among individuals.

Market Capitalism

Capitalism, as we know the enterprising system today, is mixed with varying degrees of individualism and collectivism, individual freedom and individual patterned direction. The market oriented economy, underpinned by specialization of economic activities and a monetized and sophisticated exchange mechanism, must contain self-energizing, autonomous, and sensitive control arrangements which will "balance out" productive efforts of the numerous dependent specialists and coordinate and "even out" the interacting forces in market functioning.

In Adam Smith's terms:

> It is not from the benevolence of the butcher, the brewer, or the baker that we expect our dinner but from their regard for their own self-interest. We address ourselves, not to their humanity, but to their self-love, and never talk to them of our

necessities, but of their advantages. (Adam Smith, *Wealth of Nations*, Modern Library Edition, 1937, p. 14.)

Self interest of profit-seeking entrepreneurs, then, provides the motivating force guiding producers in the market oriented economy. Controls over economic activities and coordinating "evening out" forces are concepts built into free enterprising and market oriented economic functioning.

MARKET INFRASTRUCTURE

Within the institutional structure of the market, the economic phenomena of supply and demand are coordinated and "balanced out" through functioning of the price mechanism. Clearly, however, in the exchange process goods and services must ultimately exchange for goods and services. When the talk and planning is about community or regional economic development, this clear-cut exchange relationship cannot be ignored. The production of goods and services creates income which in turn grants the producer a claim on the production of others through the exchange process as monitored by the price mechanism. Further, the exchange process is the economic growth process and, indeed, the economic lifeline of an enterprising system. The rules of the economic game hinge on the exchange process. In Joseph Schumpeter's words:

> How much meat the butcher disposes of depends on how much his customer the tailor will buy and at what price. That depends, however, upon the proceeds from the latter's business, these proceeds depend upon the needs and the purchasing power of his customer the shoemaker, whose purchasing power again depends upon the needs and purchasing power of the people for whom he produces; and so forth until we finally strike someone whose income derives from the sale of his goods to the butcher. (*The Theory of Economic Development*, 1934, p. 7.)

MARKET VALUE THEORY

Clearly illuminated by Schumpeter's words is the notion that the economic worth of a man is directly measured by the exchange value of his production. The economic worth of the "system" is determined by how well it lubricates, facilitates, and sustains exchange processes full circle from the butcher through the community and back to the butcher. Further than this, beyond the strictly economic, Adam Smith formulated a different theory of economic activity and human value relationships. In Smith's exposition the individual's search for his own self interest best served the economic interests of the society. The marketplace, typical of so many human institutions in the eighteenth and nineteenth centuries, was endowed by men with a theological value—the market became a vehicle through which God worked his will.

DECISION-MAKING IN ECOLOGICAL MOVEMENT

Economic ecology provides an analytical approach to those decision-making processes applicable to man's adaptation to the changing market and to his changing environment. Community leaders, including those of business and government, are quite aware of their roles as decision-makers. Few, however, are able to explain how they reach decisions. The issue, it seems, rests on an understanding of what it is that is subject to decision. Clearly, decision is the selection of a particular behavior pattern from a set of alternative behavior patterns. Further, decision-making must be analyzed within the structure of the organized entity itself.

In discussing decision-making theory Simon defines rationality: "the selection of preferred behavior alternatives in terms of some system of values (perhaps $) whereby the consequences of behavior can be evaluated."

On the basis of this definition, he then comments:

> It is impossible for the behavior of a single isolated individual to reach any high degree of rationality. The number of alternatives he must explore is so great, the information he would need to evaluate them so vast that even an approximation to objective rationality is hard to conceive. Individual choice takes place within an environment of 'givens' . . . premises that are accepted by the subject as bases for his choice; and behavior is adaptive only within the limits set by these 'givens'. (Herbert A. Simon, *Administrative Behavior*, 2nd ed., 1957, p. 75.)

Simon points out that all decision is a matter of compromise. The behavior finally selected from a set of alternatives never permits a complete or perfect achievement of objectives, but is rather the best solution available under the circumstances. Compromise, rather than consensus, marks economic system developments in the United States.

Ecology in Political Economy

Calvinism and the Puritan ethic endowed Smith's market system with a new sanctification. A man's spiritual worth became identified with his economic worth. However, not all men agreed with Smith. Economic reality did not mesh well with Smith's theory. As it turned out, it was not the market that revamped economic and human relationships, but rather society acting and seeking social reforms both outside and within the market structure. Robert Owens and the Utopians sought redress from long hours, unsanitary conditions, child labor, and preventable social conditions that degraded human dignity. Karl Marx made a more direct and militant response to the problem of social evils. Fabianism, while embracing a philosophy of collectivism, was a moderate doctrine. Socialism was to be secured by peaceful economic and social means based on democratic processes and institutions. Public awareness of the need for correction of social evils would be aroused through education.

Business unionism as it has developed in the United States was illustrated by Samuel Gompers' testimony before the Congress. Gompers stated: "What the unions want is 'more'. More, that is, of the economic fruit labor helps produce." Sumner Slichter broadened the union role as serving two purposes: (1) that of determining the price of labor, and (2) the introduction of civil rights into industry, i.e., management by rule rather than by arbitrary and unilateral decision.

Rules and the Economic Game

As ecological movements in market system development are observed, the basics of decision are apparent. When one asks, what is it that is directly and immediately subject to choice and decision by the decision-making agency, whether that agency be private firm management or a government legislative body, the response must be in terms of the rules governing human behavior. When proposals were made to modify market functioning (to alleviate or temper social disadvantages) the proposal inevitably took the form of a change in the set of rules governing men in their economic oriented endeavors. In the sense that a significant change in the rules governing behavior changes the basic "givens" themselves, an entirely new economic, political, and social game of human life styles emerges. Together, business unionism and government's legislation and involvement in economic endeavors have significantly modified many past social and economic relationships. Solutions to social problems were sought through change in the rules governing human behavior. Improvement in economic performance was sought through selection of an alternative set of rules. This concept applies with equal appropriateness to firm executives seeking to improve their quality control procedures or their merchandising endeavors, to the nation's football coaches meeting to make football a better game to play and watch, to legislators considering broadly-based problems of national defense, intergovernmental grants-in-aid, or measures to improve financial and economic stability, and to metrogovernment officials pondering the urban problems of traffic, housing, and air pollution.

The infrastructure of the market as considered in this work indicates that the market institution is man-made. As such, the social good must be the responsibility of *someone* who writes the rules governing behavior in the market and not merely *something* that is an impersonal market functioning. Certain nagging questions provide an interlocking thread which can be traced throughout this analysis: Whose responsibility? How much responsibility? Terms such as social responsibility, corporate community citizenship, social overhead capital, and public health which are commonplace today would have been meaningless in Adam Smith's time.

Economic ecology moves ultimately to present day integration of public-private sector endeavors and mutual interests. Social forces, absent from Smith's economic theory, are injecting themselves forceably into economic affairs. The market as a man-made institution can be modified to embrace new environmental requirements while retaining and strengthening individual freedom and motivation through the economic life styles maintained. In effect, the nation has arrived at a point in time which requires decision if the urban society is not to fall prey to its own polluted environment. Recognizing behavior patterns in issues requiring decision is the key to ecological movement.

.. 2 ..

Ecology of Economic Organization

With the evolution of a market oriented economic system, customs and traditions of the past which assured the "making of a living" were largely discarded. Uncertainty, risk, and reward for entrepreneurship appeared as dominant phenomena of the economic system. Adam Smith's articulation of his observations formed the basis of the evolving rules of the game in a free-enterprising system and its discipline. As a discipline, and with considerable preciseness within stated premises, economics attempted to explain and predict human actions in given economic situations and within given system parameters. The free market, with its built-in institutional automaticity governing and guiding human economic decision-making and behavior, seemed a wondrous discovery.

Classical doctrine isolated, defined, and conceptualized the producer goods used in the production process, i.e., land, labor, capital, and entrepreneurship. Their use in the production process yielded income to each factor respectively, rent to land, wages to labor, interest to capital, and profit to the entrepreneur for risks assumed and for his innovations in the utility production process.

Adam Smith—A Critic As Well As Champion of Capitalism

A fundamental proposition postulated in Adam Smith's *Wealth of Nations* is that in the economic system governed by the market the entrepreneur is led by an invisible hand to promote an end which was no part of his intention. In laissez faire doctrine the individual quest for selfish gain (profits) maximizes, at the same time, the benefits to society. Higher levels of employment and income are by-products of firm economic actions rather than targeted ends. Self-interest as the spark and individual freedom and creativity as the means provide the classical formulation for the economic ecological transformation to the market oriented economy.

Smith cannot, however, be regarded simply as a blind champion of capitalism. In his professorial status he was an objective, dispassionate observer of matters economic. He did not blindly stick to the theoretical mold he had fashioned and argue that self-interest always and necessary coincides with the common good. Said Smith, "Profit hunger conflicts with public interest in that it always aims at monopoly." He defined monopoly as "infamous covetousness which does not shrink from terrorization and crime." And Smith's widely quoted observation: "People of the same trade seldom convene without their entertainment ending in a conspiracy against the public or a scheme for an increase of price." Smith's treatise reflects recognition of underlying economic change and sets forth a plea for the enforcement of competition as being the providential or natural economic arrangement which assures reconciliation of private and public interest.

MARKET AUTOMATICITY

There are many small buyers and sellers unable to exert sufficient market power individually so as to influence market price. There is freedom of exit and entry by firms to the market; no personal preferences or relationships are present; the product is homogeneous; and price is set by the free interacting play of supply and demand forces. Under such conditions, the most goods will be produced at the lowest possible price, that is at cost. "For cost is the natural position of price, inasmuch as price is drawn back to it by expansion or contraction of output, whenever the price rises or falls under that equilibrium position." (Eduard Heimann, *History of Economic Doctrines*, 1945, p. 66.)

Competitive price theory and market automaticity can be summarized in two propositions. First, market price is determined by the ratio between demand and supply, and therefore rises and falls with that ratio. Price in this stance reflects relative measurements of value. In the second proposition, a rise in the price of a product increases the gain (proceeds) to be made by its sale and thereby encourages entrepreneurs to increase output. Falling prices, on the other hand, involve losses to the producer or seller and make it psychologically and financially impossible to con-

tinue production on the previous scale. Thus the ups and downs
in the price barometer reflecting the variations in demand for
any given commodity or service stimulate a corresponding expansion or contraction of output offered for sale in the marketplace. In this way, price tendencies reflect the relative positions
of the marginal buyer and the marginal seller. The ratio of demand
to supply moves along toward equilibrium and market clearance.
Price is, accordingly, a homeostatic regulatory mechanism which
directs, coordinates, and limits economic actions in a free, private, decentralized economic system. Competition assures that
the "normal" or "natural" nexus around which price fluctuates
is cost. Above cost, price and proceeds spell profit; below cost,
price and proceeds reflect loss. Where competition equilibrates
demand and supply at cost the market is cleared and homeostatic
stability is attained at least momentarily. This tentative conditioning is inserted because just as supply follows demand in direction
and degree, so does demand follow changes in people's income,
tastes, and preferences, and the relative prices of other goods and
services. These factors also augur of homeostatic automaticity.

FROM MODEL TO REALITY—THE BUSINESS ENVIRONMENT

Price competition is an institutional arrangement depicting
economic behavior, given defined parameters which establish the
rules of the game. Because Smith's assumptions are impossible of
attainment, pure competition never really existed anywhere in
the business community. Nonetheless, the broad general scheme
did infiltrate men's minds and still lingers in recondite abstraction.

Let's go back a century or so to the decade preceding the War
Between the States. Business firms were typically the small owner-
operated proprietorship, serving a local market. Each typical entrepreneur knew his customers, his suppliers, and his employees
by their first names. He hired and fired as he pleased. He set the
price the market would bear and was "in and out" of business
with ease. Each local community lived in a state of semi-autonomous isolation. Each community of people created its own market
for goods. Local entrepreneurs responded to the market demands
for products and services and, guided by the price mechanism,
sought to satisfy market demands. As we might view the local
economy of a century ago, it is hard for one to say that business
contemporaries of the time were, as they approximated the classi-

cal model, getting the most efficient allocation of scarce resource factors in the production process.

THE ECOLOGY OF BIGNESS AND FREE ENTERPRISE

The period of Civil War provided strong impetus to change. An upsurge in the demand for goods and a widening of markets spurred the search for profits. With the "joint stock company" and later the corporate forms of business organization the entrepreneur increased his efficiency and importance. With passage of the 14th Amendment to the U. S. Constitution in 1864, businessmen seized upon the "due process" clause to give legal individuality, life, and continuity to the corporation. With this new organizational vehicle, the ecological adjustment of man to his economic environment was accelerated. Until the end of the era which coincided with the Great Depression of the 1930's, the business community reflected a philosophy and played a rough and tumble game of "social Darwinism," i.e., "survival of the fittest." The impetus of inventions and new technology (cheap steel, communication devices, the internal combustion engine, rubber, oil) and development of the railroads spanning the continent and linking local markets together spelled the practical death knell to the pure competitive model and its unrealistic rules of the game. Industrialization, transportation, and communication encouraged accelerated economic growth. This period (1875-1930) is oftentimes cited as the beginning of the industrial revolution in the United States and the hey day of the captains of industry.

To counter the uncertainties inherent in accelerated growth and change, cut-throat price competition, shifting markets, technological innovation, and managerial practices which placed heavier skill requirements on the entrepreneur, businessmen tied bigness through corporate power to market control. The temper of the times led to gentlemen's agreements to divide the market, to set up quota systems, to hold up prices, etc. The movement away from the market controlled economy was evident everywhere.

Smith had observed that specialization of labor was the key to productivity and the wealth of nations. Further, he said that "the specialization of labor is limited by the extent of the market." The systematizing and industrializing of transport and the development of a national railroad network not only provided an enormous outlet for investment flows in the railroad itself and in businesses along the track, but the system also broadened market organization and integrated isolated local markets into a market national in scope.

During the years 1875-1930, the seeds of economic liberalism and the industrial revolution born in England found fertile soil in the United States. Endowed with a more open society than any which man had yet conceived, Americans demonstrated the drive and inventiveness that made Yankee ingenuity a watchword the world over. (See Jacob Schmookler, "Technological Progress and the Modern American Corporation" in *The Corporation in Modern Society*, edited by E. S. Mason, 1961, p. 141-142.)

Economic Efficiency

From 1900 through 1950 market systems evolved more toward the structurally imperfect and away from the competitive. There was a multifaceted ecological departure from the competitive model, but the matters of efficiency in the production process override and explain many other considerations.

An engineering view of efficiency is commonplace. A more sophisticated view is getting the particular things produced in the right amounts that are demanded by a community of people. This is what the economic system must do. It must progress toward meeting this task or make room for another modification of rules or institutional structure, or changed arrangements and inter-relationships, or some of each. Ecological modification is a built-in and continuing facet of the economic system.

In the name of efficiency also, the system must manage to allocate resources between present and future production, between what is produced for consumption and what is invested in new capital to enlarge future output and produce higher consumption levels. There must also be present in the system an incentive to change and to develop and adopt new and more efficient methods of production. Finally, and this is key to the understanding of the economic ecological evolution we are observing, there must be ample provision for the basic research and technological developments from which spring new products and processes. The peculiar fascination of the competitive model was that given the decentralization of market power and the long-run tendency for price to equal costs of production, all the requirements for economic efficiency were met. The competitive market model provided for efficiency in allocating scarce resources; it provided for society the goods and services it desired in the right amounts; consideration was given to production for consumption now versus production of investment goods to enlarge future production of consumer goods. However, the means (savings) for implementing this latter consideration under the guise of abstinence and preference for future goods compared with present goods were grossly inadequate as economic rules governing behavior. The early market system model also provided the profit accruing to the innovator as an incentive for efficiency. However, the system made no adequate provision for the basic and applied research necessary for technological development which brings new methods and new products into existence. The ecology of this notion of economic efficiency requirements was not fully recognized until economic collapse confirmed to all that classical economic doctrine was completely inadequate to meet the economic needs of a modern industrializing and urbanizing society. By the time the new (micro) price theory of oligopolistic behavior and Income-Employment (macro) theory had been added to the economist's kit of analytical tools, the provision for basic research necessary for technological development of new processes and products had been already firmly established as an essential efficiency function in the modern corporation.

THE ECOLOGICAL MOVE TO OLIGOPOLY

With the move toward oligopoly as the dominant feature of industrial and market organization, it no longer follows necessarily that any of the former goals of social efficiency are to be realized. No longer can the "invisible hand" be a synthesizer of the public and private interest. No longer can it be postulated that most goods will be produced at the lowest possible price—that is, at cost. For cost, under the market structure of oligopoly, is no longer the "natural" position of price.

Competitive market oriented capitalism was vulnerable at two points. In the realm of ideas there was its pivotal dependence on competition, i.e., many firms, no influence on price, etc. A second essential point is that the system has to work in the real world. The rules of the game must keep the system viable. Were the assumption of competition to be undermined, at it was, it would prove a devastating blow. So also was the systems collapse in the nineteen-thirties. E. H. Chamberlin and Joan Robinson presented oligopoly, a few sellers, as something different from either competition or monopoly. A new set of analytical tools were developed to appraise the new economic structure that had replaced the traditional competitive model. Under the concept of "few," the producer can and does influence price through his influence on supply and demand. He becomes a market manipulator rather than a powerless pawn manipulated by market forces impersonally and inexorably. Surprisingly, these changed rules of the economic game and the sharply different market structure escaped acceptance by the professional economic analyst steeped in the Marshallian classical synthesis until the system's utter collapse crystallized new economic problems that could not be left for time alone to heal. New economic tools were necessary if the economic machine was to stay geared to the efficiency task of creating and distributing income and of providing the goods society desires in the right quantities at the right time and place and at the right price.

If oligopolists now had sufficient market power to hold up a price umbrella to protect themselves from the vicissitudes of price competition, they could, in theory, all live comfortably, profitably, and inefficiently together in the now impotent marketplace. Lacking the push from eager competitors, there was no longer any certainty of technical advance. Further, when sellers gain control over prices, this barometer no longer reflects the ebb tides of changes in consumer demand. Price is no longer the variable in the new economic game. Production and employment are the new variables as output is expanded or decreased to maintain price as demand fluctuates. The new game simply outlaws the use of prices as a weapon of competitive warfare. Inevitably, this convention against price competition marks the oligopolistic market structure. With price competition ruled out, competitive energies tend to concentrate on various means of persuasion. In classical theory, selling, promotional costs, advertising, and other elements of persuasion were not inherent in the structure and became an exercise in ostentatious waste. By evolution of economic organization with its resultant concentration of market power, economists steeped in classical dogma were convinced there had occurred an ecological change from a system where everything worked out for the best to a system and institutional structure where everything seemed to work out for the worst.

However, oligopoly brought with its structural development a basic supposition that the corporate form of business organization was remarkably socially efficient. The enterprizing system emanating within the market structure of imperfect competition is socially efficient in its means and ability to promote and finance basic research and to implement the fruits stemming from research. What this new game implies, then, is that there must be some element of monopoly in the market structure if the basic research necessary for progress is to be attainable. If this is a fair appraisal of the new economic game, then, oligopoly must be strongly oriented toward ecological economic change.

This traditional view shifts somewhat as eminent economists appraise the structure of the market and the concentration of the means of production. Joseph Schumpeter has asserted that the inefficiencies attributed to the changing economic structure by static theoretical analyses are relatively unimportant. The competition that counts is that which arises from innovation, new technology, new products, new organization. If Schumpeter's contention is empirically appraised in the business community, it becomes apparent that his idea of the new and important competition leads us to the doors of the large corporations.

.. 3 ..

Urbanization - Industrialization
Dynamics

In the United States, with its unique and nearly unlimited freedom of action and its vast unsettled lands "to the West," no precise *image* of American society nor of a singular national purpose became crystallized in the 19th century. The turn of the century brought with it the beginnings of a social consciousness in American society, with common bonds and identifications. World War I, the "depressed thirties," and urbanization interdependencies strengthened these bonds and demonstrated a common mutuality of interests and a broad across-the-board economic interdependency which now permeates public policy at every level. In the recent post-war period the dual experiences of accelerated urbanization and an unparalleled population explosion have generated in American society a self-consciousness as an interdependent, interacting social whole which is perhaps the single most significant phenomenon of our times. The self-image consciousness of metropolitan urban societies as autonomous groups seems at least as significant as the personal consciousness which developed in the ecological human relationship change from feudalism to the impersonal economic contract as the market system developed. An understanding of modern economic ecology and the basic processes of both economic growth and development are needed. Indeed, solutions to economic, social, and political problems in our large densely-populated urban places seem at times almost impossible in the foreseeable future. However, the growing self-consciousness of the urban-based group as an autonomous social grouping with common needs, interests, and mutual

16

interdependencies promises ultimately to overcome divergent sub-group self-interest, status quo concepts, and a reluctance to accept those ecological changes which urban environments demand. It would seem that self-consciousness and a recognition of an autonomous self-social urban image superimposed upon an extremely strong American premise of individualism and the efficacy of individual pursuit of self-interest must ultimately lead to ecological economic adjustment processes. Through movements in this direction, individual self-interest is to be served by group self-interest in an economic environment characterized by a pluralistic society. Faced with the complexities of an urban modern economic society, there exists an absolute need to develop an insight and concept of the economic system as a whole, and of metropolitan regional economies as semi-autonomous sub-systems.

URBANIZATION AND ECONOMIC ORGANIZATION

Within the environmental economic constructs of business concentration and oligopolistic organization and practice, an understanding of how the market and the forces of the price system mechanisms allocate and utilize resources is crucial to society's formulation and implementation of public policy. The advantages and disadvantages of a concentrated, oligopolistic economic market structure, minute division of labor skills, the functional dispersion of responsibilities between the several levels of governments and among private businesses, and subsequent economic behavior in a highly monetized environment are essential economic ecological considerations in appraising the dynamics of the urban place.

THE HANDICRAFT RESPONSE TO EARLY URBANIZATION AND DEVELOPMENT

Unique economic comparative advantages characterize people as well as regions. Due to differences in native abilities, interests, and acquired skills a modicum of economic specialization appears early as the market development process evolves concomitantly with the beginnings of an urbanizing community. The urban entity provides an environmental autonomy which in earlier days led to a common defense, a central market for the agricultural products produced by the surrounding regional complex, and a sense of stability as local political and economic order were introduced. A primary task of the public sector was, and is, to establish and maintain that environment conducive to private enterprising economic endeavor.

Handicraft manufacturing activities specialize early, particularly in those activities related to the provision of goods essential to minimum standards of health. In the classical tradition enterprising entrepreneurs appear in the market immediately as soon as market processes are established. Cultivators of land specialize in crop production, retain employees to work the land, and rely upon exchange in the urban marketplace to acquire the multitude of goods they want and need in exchange for their goods and services. Productivity improvements are the basis for enlargement of the trading base and for the material welfare gains stemming from specialization and exchange. Soon food processing manufactures are added either on a small household or commercial production basis. Small flour mills, sugar mills, tea factories, fruit and vegetable canneries, milk gathering, pasteurization plants, and distribution operations are organized; vegetable oil mills, jam and jelly makers, and simple pharmaceuticals—all find an enterprising entrepreneur who has spotted a need and who organizes productive factors into economic production units to fill the observed unsatisfied demand. Although tobacco products and matches do not qualify as food, the need seems almost as basic. Hence, tobacco products and matches appear as early products in the development process. The same sort of related consumer demand analysis applies to the early appearance of hard liquor and soft drinks.

Clothing is another primary need in which developmental processes appear concomitantly with an orderly urban market organization. In textile manufactures a rather orderly developmental linkage can be traced from the cotton farm to the ginning mill, then to spinning and weaving, and hence to sheets, blankets, thread, toweling, knit goods, socks, undergarments, and outer clothing to fit physical, climatical, seasonal, and status needs; and in bulk, there are simple drapery, rug, and upholstery fabrics. Leather goods also appear early in the market development process. Handicraft tanneries are sure to appear in any neighborhood that produces domestic animals. Since shoes are a fundamental need and some leather clothing items are essential, the tannery enters early into the exchange process. Further, as urbanization becomes a way of life, a growing portion of the region's population no longer have access to domestic animal skins, and other necessary supplies.

What is important at this point in the ecological context is the insight into the environmental changes which ensue from the beginnings of urbanization, market development, and early specialization in production activities. Entrepreneurs organize the factors of production, specialize their combination and use, and retain other individuals as employees whose only means of sustaining themselves is through the sale of their labor services. These entrepreneurs look to the market as their source of income, their purpose for being, and the governor of their fortunes. The rules of the economic game change pragmatically as do human relationships in the urbanization-industrialization development interaction. The ecological process sharpens and the environment quickens, as the developmental process accelerates the rate of change.

CONSUMER GOODS DIVERSIFY

As specialization augments productivity, market processes accrue higher levels of incomes, which in turn are reflected in rising demands for consumer goods and services. In our traditional market system, the consumer goods industries expand to satisfy growing and diversified product markets. Better quality products are offered the consumer (in economic jargon, superior goods more attractive to those whose incomes will permit tend to replace inferior goods). Tinned goods replace the old mason jar which housewives for generations used to preserve vegetables and fruits; frozen and packaged vegetables, fruits, and meats appear alongside and in competition with tinned goods; packaged mixes of all kinds appear on the supermarket shelves, leading the wags to observe that "any bride who can read can cook." In the same vein, books, writing papers, newspapers, magazines, ready-to-wear clothing, specialized sporting goods and clothing add to the widening range of consumer choices.

An important development in the regional market process is the response of consumer goods industries to rising demands in expanding markets. Now consumer durables make their appearance: ice boxes followed by refrigerators as electric power becomes commonplace in urban centers, together with radios, fans, lamps, washers and dryers, furniture of all kinds, bicycles, garden tools, lawn mowers, golf equipment, fishing boats and trailers, *ad infinitum*.

Basic is the free market assumption that every business firm services some market and every market is serviced by one or more firms. It is axiomatic in a viable market economy that if a demand exists for a product or service, some enterprising entrepreneur will find a way, frequently even before a minimum economic plant size is reached, to satisfy that demand. In the market economy of the United States we have seen develop the idea that "he who gets in firstest with the mostest, makes the mostest." This maxim of motivation for the entrepreneur has caused the urban center to become the mecca for small businessmen.

CAPITAL GOODS MANUFACTURE

The necessary development of the beginnings of a capital goods industry follows quickly upon the heels of development of consumer durable goods manufactures. We have seen again and again the efforts of governments of underdeveloped countries to insist upon early development of a full-fledged integrated basic steel industry whether or not the basic resource ingredients and labor skills are present. National status and prestige seem more overpowering than comparative economic advantage. Left to its own options, the market economy acts differently. Private enterprising efforts build one mole hill at a time; the mountain comes later and inexorably through the creative efforts of enterprising men capitalizing upon economic incentives and advantages.

As demands for consumer non-durable goods rise above basic minimum standards, manufacturing operations expand proportionately. As this occurs, the beginning of a capital goods industry evolves quite naturally. A growing urban market, developing manufactures to satisfy that market, higher levels of employment, and higher levels of income are associated early with the requisite surge in construction accompanying any urbanization-industrialization complex development. Very quickly in the development process, the requisite economic social-overhead base provided by the public sector comes into focus, in highways, streets, sewer and water systems, airports, hospitals, irrigation works, schools, and parks. On the publicly provided social-overhead base, the private sector develops its productive potential to satisfy consumer, business, and government demands for privately produced goods and services. With this surge of private development, construction is again in the forefront. Physical asset growth (man-made capital goods) brings to mind immediately an entire array of economic activities, many of which are local or regional in nature—the manufacture of bricks, cement, lumber, shingles, wall board, nails, plywood, pipe, and steel bars required by a burgeoning construction boom. Then, in addition to the structure itself, construction activity creates a manifold demand for products that go inside the structure: home and office furniture, equipment of every sort, textile products, water and space heaters, air conditioners, fixtures, appliances, etc. The construction boom, be it commercial, residential, or public works, creates employment, income, and subsequent demands for consumer goods and complementary capital goods. The circular nature of economic flows is once again illustrated.

The connection between industrialization, urbanization, and construction combined with the multiplier impact on income which leads to further general economic expansion deserves more precise consideration in view of today's burgeoning urban complexes.

SPECIALIZATION AND REGIONAL EXPORTS

Early in a region's developmental sequence of economic industrialization are the exploitation and export of the region's natural resources. Regional specialization and exports in the early stages of economic organization depend upon the availability and accessibility of primary raw materials. These are typically extractive industries and frequently constitute "enclave industries", on islands of economic activity only insignificantly dependent upon and interacting with the rest of the local economy. Interconnections exist only incidentally, as a limited quantity of strictly local supplies are purchased and as locally supplied labor is absorbed in the production process. At this stage of development, there exist few horizontal, vertical, or supporting linkages which spawn further economic development through significant market expansion.

At later stages of development, the regional economic organization becomes much more sophisticated. An industry or firm may be more or less resource oriented, market oriented, labor oriented, or perhaps brain-power and research oriented. Other regional and even nationally oriented industries and firms may be "service" oriented as supporting functions for the primary industries such as banking institutions and technical engineering and management consulting firms. Then of growing importance are those straight-forward more or less "pure" service-type industries that are required by the urban environment—taxis, hotels, motels, restaurants, theaters, convention centers, major league athletic stadiums, and the like. Insofar as "services" are sold to and consumed by tourists or visitors to the metro-region, the effect is analogous in economic impact to the physical export of products. Insofar as economic development and urbanization proceed hand-in-hand, the export dependency of the manufacturing sector and much of the service sector, as growing sources of regional income, remain crucial to the region's economic health.

With regard to manufacturing, economically-sized industrial operations must depend upon export sales beyond the regional complex limits for sufficient market demand to justify and support the size and specialized technology required by efficient modern production methods. Similarly, the pure service industries depend upon a multitude of economic and related attractions, such as climate, to sustain high-capacity utilization of productive facilities. In the same frame of reference, England is an industrialized-urbanized economy which must export to survive. The same principles apply even more critically to a regional metropolitan complex too small to specialize and be supported by an autonomous self-sufficient localized regional market.

The Economic Momentum Duality

Urbanization-industrialization-business economic developments have followed a fairly typical market oriented pattern. A constant problem is that of maintaining *momentum* in the economic growth processes. This problem is inherent in the economic system itself and is reflected in the dual responsibilities assigned the private sector in our enterprising economy:

1. firms are expected to supply society with the goods and services desired in about the right quantities at about the right prices.

2. firms are relied upon to create and distribute income among those who contribute to the production process.

Analysis of urban economic organization and functioning centers frequently upon a broadening and articulation of these dual economic responsibilities. The urban environment requires many utilities for collective consumption not within the scope of market pricing processes; for example, no user price is easily attached to such public services as streets, schools, or sewers. Also, the public sector has been forced by political pressure to move into many areas of joint economic-social concern as the private sector fails to meet fully the responsibility of creating and distributing sufficient income to meet the needs of a vibrant and viable urban economy.

The Composite Urban Economy

The many problems emanating from urbanization processes are self-reinforcing and become proportionately more service oriented and complex as population density continues to increase. The decay of central business districts, the spread of adjoining slums, the despoiling of sprawling suburbs coincident with the urbanization-industrialization patterns of development, and the concentration of widely heterogeneous populations in urban asphalt jungles require a hard-headed practicality and insight if regional economic health is to be maintained.

In recent years the face of the political economy has been altered by accelerated demographic movements toward primary urban centers. Ecological developments have tempered whole economic environments of semi-autonomous regions. All too often regions and entire communities experience loss of business firms, unemployment and loss of skills, and an inability to uplift their economic performance to meet the highly specialized demands of dynamic labor and product markets.

Urban centers cannot close their doors to those in-migrating people whose personal equipment and development are so often totally inadequate to meet the demands of an advancing technology in the urban job market. Metropolitan complexes must be flexible enough to accept these migrants and to embark upon programs designed to seek solutions to the social and economic problems created. Central to any solution or more aptly "set of solutions" is a plan or program of action specifically designed to maintain a proper balance between labor force growth, job creation, and income flows. The urgent need to recognize and implement policies adequate to fill the need for job creation and income distribution must concern public and private leadership at all levels, in all regions, and in all industries. Ecologically the economic system is being modified, and the demands placed upon the system are becoming more exacting and complex. Sound economic health is an essential requisite of both national and regional economic well-being.

Economic Balance: Some Propositions

Urban leaders must coordinate their efforts if they are to maintain regional economic balance. An effective approach for sustaining a working equilibrium between labor force growth and job creation and income growth must encompass the macroeconomic variables of population, employment, labor force, and income. Again, the key lies in economic flows.

It is desirable that the labor force of any urban complex grow in balance with the ability of the complex to provide employment for its people living in a highly monetized environment. Rapid and/or significant deviations from such a desired balance lead inexorably to complex social and economic problems of imbalance. Local action can counter deviations from balanced equilibrium conditions within acceptable limits. Local leaders need to recognize and understand the nature of local economic flows and the interacting multiplier impact of urban growth, industrialization, and construction on basic job creation processes with its primary, secondary, and tertiary effects upon income growth and distribution.

Interacting forces such as technological innovation, changing demand requirements in product and labor markets, and resource adequacy and availability are continually shifting the focus of business opportunity. These developmental processes of interacting forces, coupled with unique regional comparative advantages, enhance the mobility of people and economic activities within and between autonomous economic regions. In the short run, these forces can be minimized using today's technology, managerial skills, and public and private coordinated efforts. While metroeconomic regions can do little to alter basic and fundamental endowments, they can take decisive steps to improve the corrective market processes that work to balance labor force participants with job and income growth. Central factors such as time lags in the adjustment process, failures in information dissemination concerning economic opportunities, differences in unique comparative advantages and competition between regions for economic industrialization and business development, differences in the adequacy and provision of urban social-overhead capital facilities, and differing incidence of adaptation to or adoption of innovations may all, to a degree more than is generally recognized, be amenable to action by coordinated and cooperative efforts of metropolitan regional public and private leadership. In this instance, community leaders' understanding of basic relationships emanating from basic urbanization-industrialization-business development processes and the various economic flows stemming from these processes can with purposive action make the economic system "work for them". Man is no longer a pawn to be tossed about idly from wave to trough in the economic seas. Man can now chart his way; economic development occurs on purpose; urban economic health is attainable through purposive and continuing coordinated public-private actions; in a highly monetized economy the choice of striving for sound urban economic health presents a Hobson's Choice, which means no choice if the existing economic system and basic social structure are to stand.

.. 4 ..

Urban Dynamics and Small
Business Enterprise

ADAM SMITH sought to explain "the invisible hand" which "motivated the private interests and passions of men" and which led businessmen in that way "which is most agreeable to the interests of the society as a whole." (See Robert Heilbroner, *The Worldly Philosophers*, pp. 53-56.) The economic system automatically assured "the greatest material well-being for the greatest number."

Since the turn of the century, and particularly during the postwar decades, small business enterprise has been enmeshed in disturbing environmental challenges. With rapid urbanization, widespread technological and organizational innovation, dynamically productive basic research, and the centralization of large agglomerations of economic and political power, accelerated environmental change has become a central fact in economic processes which concern the small business enterpriser in the urban market place. The significant changes in the market structure have accentuated the uncertainties of small business enterprise. Notwithstanding growing limitations placed upon the market mechanism by the spreading "mixed" aspects of the economic system, the market mechanism continues to dominate and guide the economy of small business enterprise. The market as a mechanism supporting and facilitating small business enterprise goes far beyond merely providing for the production and exchange of goods and services. Indeed, the enterprise system guided and governed by forces of the market system sustains a way of life. Small business enterprise economics rests upon individualism, freedom of action, and a willing consensus for collective, community action when such collective action meets the tests of democratic processes.

These aspects of economic, social, and political liberalism are
present today in greater measure than man has ever experienced
in any previous period. With complete candor, the American
economic society continues to move forward, to inquire, to search,
to experiment, to modify, to compromise. This is the way viable
economic systems are made. Uncertainties are inherent in the
ecology of environmental change, for small business enterprise
requires adapting to the new rules of the economic game being
played.

Economic Architecture of the Market Place

An understanding of the world of small business enterprise
requires consideration of the economic architectural structure
of the business community—the relative "mix," roles, and relationships of large and small firms in the market dominated system.
At the end of 1964, the Department of Commerce estimated the
existence of some 4,900,000 business firms in the United States. Of
these, the mix was such that some 4,640,000 firms were classified
as small. This terminology implies that individual entrepreneurship
of the prime decision making center can be pinpointed. As a
general rule of thumb, the Small Business Administration uses a
yardstick defining small firms as those employing 500 or fewer
employees.

The SBA terminology and yardstick hardly meet rational defi-
nitions of "small" business enterprise. Across-the-board in American industry some $20,000 plus investment per employee is the
rule. In SBA terms, then, a firm employing 500 employees and
using a $10,000,000 investment in technology and facilities qualifies
as small. A more realistic vantage point is needed to properly
discern the architectural structure of the urban business community.
About 75 percent of *all* business concerns employ four or fewer
employees; 90 percent employ ten or fewer employees. These
are the small business enterprisers of Smithian doctrine exemplify-
ing individual entrepreneurship, initiative, and the personalized
quest for profits. Also, in this regard, it is empirically realistic
to recognize that some 82 percent of all commercial and industrial
business firms have a tangible net worth of $35,000 or less.

Some Theoretical Implications of Firm "Mix"

A discerning look at the "mix" of firms in the developed
economic architectural structure clearly depicts the imbalance
between the existing quantitative and qualitative exercise of market

power. Gardner Means, in recent testimony before the Congress, estimates that the 100 largest manufacturing firms own, operate, and control 58 percent of all the assets—the machines, tools, equipment, facilities, and the like—used in the manufacturing sector in the United States. Economists have not yet satisfactorily captured this imbalance in their theoretical constructs depicting firm behavior. Oligopoly theory (or theories), beginning with Edward Chamberlain and Joan Robinson in the thirties, provides a bridge of sorts from classical doctrine to present day theory (or theories) of firm behavior in the market place. Current theory explaining firm behavior attempts to encompass all motivations and behaviors of the large, the middle-sized, and the small firms using one set of analytical and theoretical tools. Most certainly oligopoly theory aids policy makers in better understanding the corporate institution, its behavior in the market, and the impact of its concentrated economic powers on the market.

Such theory as we have, however, is not universally accepted; nor does it help us move toward a realistic understanding of firm decision-making or market behavior of the large, conglomerate private enterprise nor of its counterpart, the large public corporation (TVA, post office), nor of the behavior patterns and motivations of the middle-sized, small, and very small business firms. By grouping all sizes of firms together in a single "set" of theoretical parameters explaining their market behavior, economists are merely adapting that literary device of the simile which forces an alien notion into an equation with a familiar concept in order to isolate and build on some identifiable common factor.

The Small Enterprise Game

The role small business enterprise can play, and indeed the role small firms are expected to play, is largely predetermined. The "rules of the business game" are structured in the market place by big business practices and controls exercised over market functioning. Other rules, the direct "do's and don'ts of the small business game, are written by units of governments. Rules change and cause many uncertainties in the economic fortunes of small business enterprisers. The small business road is often filled with pitfalls, for the rules of the economic game are most frequently made more or less unilaterally outside the sphere of small enterprisers' influence.

The ecological trend in the changing rules of the economic game has tended to make small business enterprise operations and opportunities increasingly subordinate to or tied to large corporate organizations. However, any reports that small business is declining are dead wrong. Neither singly nor in combination have economies of scale, accelerated merger actions, massive government procurement, automation, taxation, urbanization, or urban renewal reduced the small businessman to insignificance. Enterprising men continue to appear almost everywhere in the business communities. A dynamic and urbanizing economy has compensated for the debilitating impacts of growing business concentration and the subsequent self-enhancing exercise of private market power. Dynamic aspects of the economic system has postponed what could become, should growth rates slow down, an increasingly adverse economic system characteristic limiting "independent" small business enterprise opportunities. The traditional theory, "find a need and fill it," of small enterprise success is largely an anachronism for small "independent" business entrepreneurs. In an increasingly complex and sophisticated economic environment "big business" with its professional research facilities is most apt to "discover" the need, is most able to finance the innovation, and is most likely to fill it.

The Franchiser

The trend away from the "independent" entrepreneur of classical theory is apparent in the urban market place. We are aware of the exceedingly rapid expansion of franchised operations such as hamburger stands, pizza parlors, waffle houses, rug cleaning services, automatic laundries, automobile dealers, name-brand motels and restaurants (over 2,000 different franchise opportunities are estimated). The success of the "chain" of franchisers is based on large and complex organization. The success of the individual entrepreneur is based on conformity and adherence to "tried and proven" production, selling, promotion, and pricing practices. Essentially the individual franchiser is strait-jacketed. His theoretical entrepreneurial role of creative decision-maker is notably different in pragmatic day-to-day operations. His investment policies are predetermined (even as to color and shape: note the Howard Johnson chain); his employment needs are determined by his predetermined investment in facilities and equipment; his wage policies are prescribed by government, unions, or by big business firms competing in the marketplace, and he is allowed little or no deviation; his product is rigidly defined and controlled; his prices also are set in the franchise mold. The emphasis is on "own your own business" and you can for as little as $1,000 on up to $1,000,000 or more arrange to market a product, sell a service, or buy a franchise for an area and sublease it. Whereas in theory the small business enterpriser is a rugged individualist, in today's franchised world the small business entrepreneur jumps headlong into the current of economic conformity.

THE SATELLITE

Opportunity for many small business enterprisers is found in a tie-in with large firms. General Motors reportedly has more than 50,000 satellite firms as suppliers, dealers, etc. These contractual tie-ins also emphasize "own your own business" and have provided a broad path to private entrepreneurship in a viable economic system arrangement. However, the contractual agreements are commonly so all-inclusive as to establish quite definite parameters around the satellite decision-making process. The rules of the economic game are unilaterally imposed, specified, and enforced by the economic power center. The power wielded in this instance has been criticised by economists of the United Auto Workers Union, who charge the "big three" with monopolistic practices in limiting freedom of action of satellite firms in such seemingly internal policies as investments, wages, production techniques, market options, and the like. And significantly, in the ecological sense of system change, the UAW charge includes the exercise of definite controls over allowable profits and rates of return on investment for satellite firms. Again, the rules of the economic game for small business enterprisers are shaped by big business decisions and practices. Large firms, as a matter of policy, constantly evaluate expansion plans in terms of alternatives; should a new addition be internally financed and operated or should a tie-in with at least partially independent investment by small enterprisers be the organizational format used? In this instance again, entrepreneurial theoretical economic behavior bears little resemblance to the behavior one observes empirically. "Opportunity cost," on alternative actions of behavior, govern the entrepreneurial enterprising man more than any quest to "maximize profits."

THE SMALL BUSINESS MARKET ENVIRONMENT

At every turn, in every endeavor, in any type of manufacturing, distribution, or commercial activity, and in every market in which he buys or sells, the "little fellow" is in direct competition with the larger firm and is subject to the rules of the game and economic conditions established by the centers of private economic power. With little or no leverage ability in his limited market, the small business enterpriser faces the facts of economic life. His costs of production are always price determined and can never be price determining; that is, he can never significantly influence the supply-demand relations existing in his market for his product or service. His monopoly power is essentially non-existent. To stay in business, the small enterpriser is hard put to remain "independent." He is unable to exercise the freedom of movement to maximize profits, to minimize costs, to differentiate his product, or to initiate or prevent changes in the rules of the business game. In addition, the more highly organized a market structure becomes, the more exacting are the limitations placed upon the small enterpriser. Most often the choices are few: join as a franchiser, amalgamate, become a captive satellite, or retire as an "independent" from an increasingly competitive small business environment.

A Factor in Motivation

Kept in a system focus, the concept of maximization of profits gives way in the small business outlook to a concept of economic opportunity cost. For some two million self-employed enterprisers with annual net income below $5,000, the constant day-by-day alternative consideration is "shall I try to go it alone for one more day, or week, or month, or shall I take a job with a firm from 8 a.m. to 5 p.m." These entrepreneurs represent about forty percent of all firms in the business community, the marginal businesses that come and go rapidly. As a rule of thumb, for each nine new businesses that are started each year, eight disappear after an average life of one to three years. It is estimated that 90 percent of small business failures in the 1950 decade were due to inept management. On the other hand, the rapid growth of the franchised, strait-jacketed, conformist small business enterpriser has tended to improve efficiency, reduce waste in the utilization of resources, and improve service to the society. In any event, the nature of the economic system has undergone another ecological change.

Small Business and the Economic Interstice

In the urban complex, the small business entrepreneur has found both promise and problems. Growing population, rising income levels, increasing functional specialization, and an augmented economic interdependency have combined to create unbounded service opportunities for enterprising men. Urban economists note that small business enterprise contributes significantly to the resiliency, the diversity, and the continuity of economic flows in the urban place. Small firms mesh horizontally and vertically with large firms in manufacturing, merchandising, transportation, construction, and in finance and professional activities as well. Over the broad range of diverse services required by firms, households, and a dense concentration of larger numbers of employees in the urban place, the small firm fills essential specialized economic niches. This is the theory of the economic interstice.

Along with the growing concentration in manufacturing, and widening of the horizontal linkages in merchandising, the small business enterpriser has survived because of (1) a healthy and growing economy, (2) the franchise development, (3) the satellite arrangement, and (4) in a few remaining less organized, less complex industries as a marginal independent, or (5) in some narrow specialty area with insufficient market potential to attract big business investment or to promise long term growth.

The O.E.O. and Small Business Development

The economic interstice idea is inherent in the Economic Opportunity Act of 1964 which articulates a small business philosophy reminiscent of the classical concept with its traditional ring. "The United States can achieve its full economic and social potential only if every individual has the opportunity to contribute to the full extent of his capabilities and to participate in the workings of our society. It is, therefore, the policy of the United States to eliminate the paradox of poverty in the midst of plenty in this nation by opening to everyone the opportunity for education and training, the opportunity to work, and the opportunity to live in decency and dignity." Title IV of the Act provides the means for new training and employment opportunities; means to assist in the establishment, preservation, and strengthening of small business concerns, and to improve the managerial skills employed in such enterprises; and means to mobilize for those objectives private as well as public managerial skills and resources. Through the Act, the federal government provides a new source of capital funds and provides management training and consulting guidance for enterprising men seeking to make their own jobs through small business enterprise. The empirical success of implementation

of the Act in regard to small business development is secondary
to the philosophy expressed and to impending economic system
modifications. Provisions of the Act suggest a determined effort
to counteract certain of the economic trends, uncertainties, and
changes in the business community and dynamic urban market
structures which have had an adverse impact on independent businessmen.

Small business enterprise is a vital and dynamic force in our
economy. Preservation of a dynamic small business enterprise becomes essential to the preservation of a private, market-oriented,
free enterprise economic system, and indeed, to a way of life.
It is in this frame of reference that the opportunity for all
Americans to participate in economic processes must be provided
in the evolving economic system by holding open the door of
opportunity and by enhancing the resiliency of small business
enterprise in the urban place.

Smallness Fills an Interstice

The rapid demographic movement to the city has been ac-
companied by an extraordinary shift toward employment in services. Fortunately for the enterprising man, the scale and advantages
of size frequently remain with the more personalized small business unit. The local focus is often to the small enterprising man's
advantage in many aspects of providing services to households or
businesses where personalized human relationships or skills constitute a more important prerequisite than the nominal money capital
required in small enterprise operations. The rise of wide ranging
service industries necessary to a highly dependent urbanized people
tends to favor development of an almost unlimited number of
small business service opportunities and self-employment. The
economic interstices created by highly urbanized, highly monetized
environments are being filled in a variety of ways. The more
specialized and varied the needs of households, businesses, and
governments become in the super-urbanized metropoli, the more
economic interstices will be created. As they are filled, self-employment opportunities for enterprising men are realized. At the
same time, equally enterprising men seek to organize and exercise control over developing markets for products and services
through franchise, product differentiation, or other methods. The
economic system must encompass all such endeavors and sustain
their dynamism if urban economic health is to be attained and
sustained.

Small Business Development in the Urban Place

Rapid urbanization provides numerous gaps in the broad economic structure which small firms can fill. Economists can, however, make only an educated guess as to the number, type, size, and scope of small business enterprise services needed at any given time or at any stage or size of urban development. Little empirical knowledge is at hand to demarcate with any precision the private business utilities required to support a given size urban population. Nor is much known as to how the requirements and hence business opportunities proliferate as population size and density rises. Even such seemingly obvious inquiries as "how many service stations?", or "how many barber shops?", or "how many public parking lots and garages?" are in the city cannot be readily or accurately answered. Beyond such simple queries, if one is searching for such indices of measurement as numbers of employees by skill classification, capital investment figures by firm, industry, and type, or perhaps groupings of firms by industrial classifications, or the numerous varieties of business supporting tie-ins or related interdependencies, only fragmented data is available on the local scene. Partial data listings such as those compiled by the U. S. Department of Commerce and local Chambers of Commerce provide bases for an educated guess, not much else. The 75 percent of firms with four or fewer employees—more often than not members of the owners family—do not usually belong to local chambers and are sampled only scantily by the usual data sources. One difficulty of business census is, of course, that small business mobility is high, the marginal firms come and go.

Interstices in the CBD

Central Business Districts in the various metropoli follow quite standardized development patterns. Essentially, as an economic nerve center for the region, the CBD tends to become a conglomerate of white collar activities. The CBD is the financial center with its banking institutions, savings and loans, finance companies, stock brokers, factoring companies, the SBA, and related type financial institutions. The CBD is also the site of home or branch office headquarters, the administrative centers for insurance companies, public utilities, professional firms, and medical office buildings and services. Similarly, government offices are in the center of downtown in the CBD. The federal office buildings, the post office, the various agencies, city hall and its annexes,

and the county courthouse in the urbanized counties are typically
downtown.

Clearly identified with this centralized concentration of thousands of white collar employees are the wide variety of service
firms where there is the "opportunity" to serve the CBD community. Commercial interests are such that the "big" stores—
Macy's, Marshall-Fields, Neiman-Marcus, and Rich's—are located
in the center of downtown. Accompanying commercial establishments are the innumerable specialty shops which supplement the
huge department stores and cater to the white collar group:
men's shops, women's dress shops, toddlers' shops, shoe stores,
restaurants, cafeterias, coffee shops, parking lots, auto dealers,
service stations, drug stores, variety stores, furniture and appliance
stores, general merchandise stores other than department stores,
and always one finds a few general food stores and specialty food
stores, laundry and dry cleaning establishments, tailor shops,
shoeshine parlors, barber shops, beauty salons, and many more.
The list is interminable. Although chain operations are prevalent
in much of the CBD business activity, there are a great many
marginal individualized firms which rise and fall with each economic pulse beat of the CBD. The enterprising men have an amaz-
ing sensitivity to needs and to change according to the needs of
the group they serve. Their economic ups and downs reflect
directly the economic health of the CBD and its transition and
modification as metropolitan size and density continues to rise.

Interspersed throughout the CBD and always close by are
the hotels and motels. Closely allied with the hostelry service, the
entertainment world is prominent with theater marquees, night
clubs with neon lights, the legitimate theater, the community audi-
torium, art center, sports stadium, and the like. As the economic
architecture of the community is designed and constructed by the
main centers of economic activity, the interstices are again filled
by enterprising men ranging from the popcorn man near the
theater to the con man in his multifarious roles which skirt the
edge of legality and sometimes go beyond. However, speaking
economically, the "night life" of any great city is a source of income which is sizeable in its impact, and it provides the attraction
of entertainment, theatre and other cultural advantages which are
present only in large urban places.

Research to Foster Small Business Development

A first step in small business promotion and development in

the urban complex is to understand supportive business relationships and to design a model of the economic architectual structure. We do not know and can only guess at this time the scope,
the variety, and the diversity of small business enterprise necessary to meet the needs of a super-urbanized community with its
specialized, interdependent people living in a highly monetized
environment. Only through meticulous research and analysis can
the thousands of economic interstices offering opportunity for
enterprising men be identified. We know that the small business
firm typically services a special, particularized clientele or geographical market. A delineation of these markets in geographical
terms, income levels, functional supportive performances, products
or services, and clientele would indicate the processes involved in
meshing economic flows, the diversity of products and services
offered an urban population group, and would greatly assist in
the "spotting" of small business development opportunities. From
such analyses would come a better understanding of those dynamics of urban change that both create and destroy small marginal
enterprisers.

Political Posture for Enterprise Development

Particularly at the local level, governments and businesses act
in full partnership to meet the public and private needs of an
urban population. Governments provide what consensus decides
are public goods. Governments also create the basic organization
for economic activity and set forth direct rules of the game. Public
services and the social overhead capital base provided by local
governments are absolutely critical economic factors to local
business enterprise. In numerous instances, what the city does
or does not do can spell survival or failure for the firm. In the
area of housing the spread of neighborhood slums spreads contiguous slums in the business community which services those
households. Freeway construction improving access to suburbia
with its deluxe, well-furbished shopping centers and ample parking
space tends to increase competitive pressure and sometimes to
create untenable conditions for existing businesses in the downtown section. Housewives who spend most of the family income
are unwilling to face heavy traffic to shop downtown except occasionally on a "day-out" basis at the big central *name* stores. With
the suburban shopping centers sharply invading their market, the
downtown businessmen have adapted and specialized their efforts.
The changing function of the central city, the tendency to become

heavily oriented toward government, finance, insurance, company headquarters office-type operations, entertainment, hostelry and the concomitant dense concentration of white collar and professional people in a limited geographical space spells economic interstice opportunity for many service-type enterprises and a dead-end-of-the-road for others. Uncertainties facing small business enterprise are omnipresent in creeping as well as dynamic conditions of urban environmental change.

The question, which remains essentially unanswered, is what happens to the displaced small businesses? Courtland Street in Atlanta today, for example, is lined with elegant and very busy motels contiguous to the busy central business district, a high rise apartment building, a number of new office buildings housing insurance companies, and a new municipal Coliseum with parking space for the sports enthusiasts. But what about the one hundred and sixty odd small businesses displaced by the renewal effort in this instance: What happened to them and to their proprietors? Where did they go?

The Small Business Administration, in cooperation with urban renewal authorities, endeavors to help. Special management consulting advice is given to assist in relocation. Financial assistance is also given to displaced businesses although under policies and rules which are perhaps too restrictive. But the question inevitably arises: "Does urban renewal displace small businesses and slum households for the development and benefit of big business?" Certainly, most of the "new" businesses on Courtland Street are big business units. The few in this case create far more income and employment than the previous 160 firms. But, as the environmental changes are made and as new and different economic interstices are created, the small, marginal enterprising man either adapts or drops out.

Such problems require community action and an all out effort to improve the small business climate in the urban complex. Economic health must be considered as a prime mutual objective of business and political leaders alike. Nothing short of a coordinated, metro-wide community action program can stave off deterioration, the spread of slums, and the human and economic costs involved. The relatively compact political, economic, and social structure prevailing in the typical metropolis encompasses a wide variety of neighborhoods, population characteristics, housing conditions, different types of industrial concentrations and diversifications, commercial concentrations and diversifications, and a variety of employment and small business development problems. It is because of this diversity that the theory of the economic interstice and small business development programs can provide a rational means for strengthening the economic base of the urbanized community. Title IV of the Economic Opportunity Act of 1964 and Section 502 of the Small Business Investment Act, which provides for local development companies, may prove to be effective instruments in promoting small business development and in ameliorating some of the debilitating forces gnawing at the foundations supporting enterprising men in the typical urban place.

Any impression, however, that public interest in small business development dominates, that private interest is subordinate or secondary, is wrong. The private business community relies on the meshing of economic flows and processes pertaining to suppliers, business services, governmental services, and so on. In turn, in addition to smoothing and regularizing economic flows, small business entrepreneurs also create employment, income, and consumers for products and services of the larger firms. For their own convenience, large firms decidedly want to encourage the development of small business enterprise to serve them, their employees, and the community. Banks, likewise, can see their accounts growing as small firms stabilize and multiply, as their contributions increase, as business volume rises in the community, as incomes go up, as more consumer sales stimulate further commercial activity throughout the community. In effect, the entire community benefits from the added economic strength, versatility, and diversity provided by a dynamic small business sector. This is the type effort that large business firms, economic development agencies, public utility firms, banks, chambers of commerce, and all community-oriented groups should be vitally interested in sponsoring, and working hard to develop. Too much economic development effort has been expended competing with other communities for outside firms. Insufficient effort, almost none in too many cases, has been expended in cultivating the "own back yard" of urban places through local efforts to stimulate sound development of small business enterprise, notwithstanding that such development is a crucial key to a more effective meeting of urban business, government, and household needs. Economic improvement is a mutual goal to be strived for by all progressive citizens and institutions in any metropolitan community.

GOALS FOR THE SMALL BUSINESS ENTERPRISE

As students of economic processes, let us proceed in the following manner. First, realize that the "price system," the market mechanism, the free enterprise system, and the small business enterprise environment is not the same as that "system or structure" which existed forty, twenty, or even ten years ago. Secondly, realize that our search for a policy is attuned to today's environment of dynamic urban change—flexibility is the key. Thirdly, recognize that bigness and fewness write "the rules of the game" in our economic community. Hence, private policy supporting small business development is an essential requisite. Fourth, local governments are in reality partners with large and small businesses in the economic production process and in meeting the needs of an increasingly dependent urban population.

GOALS

1. To strengthen and improve the competitive enterprise system through broadening and deepening small business development. Big business enterprise has the power and the organizational and administrative means to "rationalize" and concentrate small business activities and ventures. To do so, however, would be a further step toward fewness and an eventual invitation to regulation. Adoption and implementation of the concept of the economic interstice through the encouragement of small business development would seem to strengthen the position of big business enterprise as the center of an economic solar system providing satellite opportunities to enterprising men. Such private policy orientation would broaden the economic base to include a much larger number of enterprising participants, would strengthen motivation through the feeling of "owning one's own business" and contribute through this motivation to a fuller utilization of human skills, and finally, would contribute to the attainment of smooth, rational, and purposive economic flows throughout the community while recognizing and utilizing the partnership of self-interest encompassing all diverse groups in the urban community.

2. To keep the small business enterprise sector dynamic and expanding—to create new job opportunities, to utilize to the fullest the creativity and talents of enterprising men, to raise the level of services to individuals, households, businesses, and governments in the urban economy. Achievement of this goal requires cooperation between enterprises together with intergovernmental coordinated, community-wide action. Private and public policy

coordination can stabilize small business by regularizing the rules of the game, by crystallizing the myriad of servicing roles small businesses can play, by supporting voluntary organized actions to encourage the development of small business, and by promoting solutions to those problems inherent in urbanization which augment the uncertainties of small business enterprisers.

3. To emphasize the worth, dignity, and economic importance of small business entrepreneurship. This goal is implicit in the activities of the small business enterpriser. Management counseling, guidance, technical assistance, and formal classroom training at various levels of sophistication constitute the primary and major focus of small business development activities. Through voluntary educational means small business enterprisers can be assisted in raising the level and the competency of their operations, and through improving their economic contribution, to raise income levels of these self-employed men. The key to the dynamism of small business enterprise lies outside the influence of enterprising men themselves, for the economic game they play and the rules by which they play the game are handed to them by others. Organizational structure within the market framework can provide the architectural design, economic interstices, and the motivating forces needed to spark enterprising entrepreneurs. In this instance, private and public policies are completely compatible and share mutual objectives.

.. 5 ..

Big Business Enterprise:
an Ecological Transcendence

THE economic processes of big business and urban development are a continuation of our concepts of economic flows, urbanization-construction-employment multiplier interactions, and the creation of interstices in the architectural design of economic affairs. The late C. Wright Mills referred to men who "manage" the U. S. corporate world as the Power Elite. Mills views this group as a conservative or reactionary force. Leaders of the civil rights movement refer to this same group as "the white power structure." The late President Eisenhower, in his final and perhaps most important utterance as Chief Executive, warned the American people about a "military-industrial complex" as a group that was forcing the nation's economy toward an excessive dependence on government defense spending and, he inferred, a group that might well provoke and continue a series of cold war, half war situations for their own market growth and institutional financial security.

THE DEFENDERS

a. Sumner H. Slichter

Replying to proposals that added legal restrictions be placed on mergers so as to relieve the trend toward concentration of industrial power into a few managerial hands Slichter points out that "recent mergers have not weakened competition. On the contrary, they indirectly strengthen it because they have enabled management to build more diversified and better integrated enterprises which are more capable of reaching all parts of the domestic market, of adapting themselves to market shifts and changes in technology, of riding out the ups and downs of business, and of

supporting technological research and development." (See Sumner
H. Slichter, "In Defense of Bigness in Business," *Monopoly Power
and Economic Performance*, 1964, p. 15, edited by Edwin Mans-
field). Slichter also emphasizes the ability of large firms to carry
out basic research. "There are two principal reasons why competition tends to be rigorous when production is concentrated
among a few large concerns; one is that such enterprises keep
close track of their rank in sales and fight hard to move ahead
of rivals or to avoid being surpassed by rivals. The second reason,
and one that is rapidly gaining in importance, is the fact that
competition among large firms is being stimulated by the growth
of technological research." (*Ibid*, p. 17.)

b. Corwin D. Edwards

Edwards follows lines of reasoning developed earlier in this
text. He mentions that the big corporation assembles facilities
that are too expensive for the small company or the individual.
It can undertake systematic exploration of the variables in an
unknown field, which would not be possible for an enterprise
with a research staff too small for coordinated effort. It can
pool the risks and costs of different experiments, some of which
are likely to be profitable; whereas a small concern, unable to
determine which experiments were promising, could not afford
the chance of loss. It can spend larger sums than a small concern
for development of a new field and wait longer for operation
therein to become profitable. Thus it can explore certain technological frontiers that are not open to small enterprise. The
results of such explorations are presented to the consumer goods
and the producer goods markets continually under the brands of
the conglomerate corporations. The rivalry of these companies
in research and development is a significant instance of competition. (See Corwin D. Edwards, *Big Business and the Policy of
Competition*, pp. 88-89.)

c. Peter Drucker

In a number of publications Drucker defends the corporation
while concomitantly he poses problems seeking solutions. He
considers the big corporation as an autonomous institution and
raises the question of whether or not such bigness and autonomy—
independence from market control—is representative of the American economic philosophy. Drucker appraises the legitimacy of the
governing function of corporations over men's actions. In

Drucker's postulates, the enterprise is necessarily a governmental institution exercising vital authority over men. But, he points out, the main function and purpose of the corporation is the production of goods, not the governance of men. Its government authority over men must always be subordinated to its economic performance and responsibility. Drucker skirts, but never forthrightly enunciates, the second primary function society has relegated to the private sector dominated by big businesses—that of creation and distribution of income. He discusses big business in terms of efficiency, the production of goods for consumer satisfaction, and as socially productive institutions.

He concludes: why should any society burden itself with that complicated, delicate, and problematical institution that is enterprise, but for the fact that it is the best means found so far to produce goods for society and all its members. Having established this supposition, Drucker submits that the large corporate enterprise is a representative American institution. (See Drucker's, *The New Society*.)

THE ATTACKERS

a. George J. Stigler

Stigler's criticisms state (1) that big business possesses and uses monopoly powers; (2) big business weakens the political support for the private enterprising system; and (3) big businesses are not appreciably more efficient or enterprising than medium-size businesses. Stigler supports these criticisms by illustrations taken from corporate behavior in the business community and suggests that these cases encourage and justify bigness in labor and government. Fearful of the growing concentrations of economic market power, Stigler suggests a partial remedy to the problem. In his terms "the dissolution of big businesses is only a part of the program necessary to increase the support for a private, competitive enterprise economy, and to reverse the drift toward government control." The need to return to the Smithian atomistic industry structure and dispersion of economic market power seems to be Stigler's primary theme. He ignores what is termed new competition of technology, process, and product stemming from basic research and implementing investment. (See George J. Stigler, "The Case Against Big Business," *Fortune*, May 1952.)

b. T. K. Quinn

Mr. Quinn, a retired Vice President of General Electric Corporation, criticizes big businesses as representing the means to an end which Drucker condones. Quinn alleges that the corporate giants misrepresent economic facts when they promote the illusion that efficiency, mass production, and the specialized division of labor needed with modern technology require the conglomerates to be as big as they are. Almost every one of them is as big as it is, says Quinn, because it got the means, in one way or another, to swell to enormous size, and to take advantage of the unrestrained urge to expand, acquire, absorb, dominate, and secure its position to the maximum degree. Further, he states, in this process of acquiring bigness, individuals have been subordinated beyond recognition; the best men have often been rebuffed in favor of the least admirable; the free market has been sacrificed, bureaucracy glorified, industrial totalization established, and new independent ventures discouraged. The truth about the economy has been obscured by paid agents and publications and through the influence of lobbyists and dollars on an over-expanded big government. Huge tax write-offs and added corporate profit-financial capital funds in recent years have further entrenched monster corporations. Quinn's suggestion for creating and maintaining a wholesome climate for new ideas and new enterprises is: "the giants must be controlled and restricted and made to serve the enlightened public interest." Equity capital funds must be made available on an expanding scale to sound small business enterprise by the Federal government if no better way is found to offset the huge capital advantages of the giants; and further, tax structures must be revised to encourage the creation and growth of new ventures. We became strong, says Quinn, through the processes of getting to where we are, not in merely being where we are. Small businesses must be freed from the domination of big business. (See T. K. Quinn, *Giant Business: Threat to Democracy*, 1953, pp. 309-312.)

THE ADAPTERS

a. John Kenneth Galbraith

Galbraith, observing the pluralistic exercise of power, says, "Private economic power is held in check by the countervailing power of those who are subject to it." Discarding any naive notion of market automaticity and self-regulation, Galbraith recognizes that "Market power can be exercised by strong buyers against weak sellers as well as by strong sellers against weak buyers." These are the economic facts of life in Galbraith's context. However, Galbraith submits that in the politico-economic-social game of today it is only with great difficulty that countervailing powers are organized. Acquisition of effective countervailing powers by labor unions, retailers, consumers, farmers, and small businesses generally requires government support when such efforts occur in the big business dominated community. Galbraith postulates and envisions a growing role for government as a modifying factor in the unilateral exercise of private economic power and as a sort of arbiter in the public interest. (See Galbraith's *American Capitalism: The Theory of Countervailing Power*, 1952, pp. 113-114.)

b. The Editors of *Business Week*

"The pluralistic United States society has many centers of power in industry, government, politics, the foundations, the press, banking, labor, the intelligentsia, none of which has anything approaching absolute control." Power is also decentralized for there are quite omnipotent regional and local, as well as national, "establishments" or power groups. Further, alliances within and between these groups are uncertain and constantly shifting. In the views of the *Business Week* editors, the nature of our political democracy and the still important forces of competition in the economy curb the exercise of power by any single group or any coalition of groups. The balance of power among the various power groups keeps the economy dynamic. The public interest is concomitantly the interest of business enterprise. The new partnership developing between government and business is condoned. (See "Business and Government: A Changing Balance of Power," *Business Week*, July 17, 1965).

c. Robert L. Heilbroner

In his appraisal of the current scene Heilbroner observes: "There is the rise within our society of new elites whose competence for government is rapidly becoming of greater importance for national survival or even well-being than that of business leaders." One such elite consists of the military professionals. A second is composed of advisors from the fields of science, economics, sociology, and the academic world in general. A third includes the civil servants and the career administrators of public programs. In Heilbroner's appraisal, the abilities of big business to exploit others in the marketplace are declining as the new elites play an increasingly prominent role in education, civil rights, poverty alleviation, urban renewal, and the broader determination of federal, state, and local government fiscal and monetary policies. (See Robert Heilbroner, "The Power of Big Business," *Atlantic Monthly*, September, 1965.)

d. Joseph A. Schumpeter

Schumpeter's observations are too important to omit in this particular prospectus of ecological adaptation. In the process of creative destruction, Schumpeter observes that capitalism is by nature a form or method of economic change and not only never is but never can be stationary. The fundamental impulse, says Schumpeter, that keeps the capitalist engine in motion comes from the new consumer goods, the new methods of production or transportation, the new markets, the new forms of industrial organization that capitalist enterprise creates. It would seem most important to add that the dynamics of urbanization lend sharp power focus and added power impetus to the capitalist engine. The trauma of rapid urbanization is hardly a new phenomenon at all, for the processes of industrial motivation that constantly revolutionize the economic situation from within, incessantly destroying the old situation and incessantly creating a new situation, are, in Schumpeter's terms, the processes of creative destruction. Schumpeter is critical of economic observers who, when they appraise big business, look only at how capitalism administers existing market forces and structures. In Schumpeter's view, the more relevant observation is how big business creates and destroys them. In this destruction process the form of competition is changed and the institutional framework of the political economy is modified as rules of the game change and as the game itself is restructured. The competition coming from creative destruction is much more effective and much more important, and big business contributions to this force for change bring improvement and benefits to society. (See Schumpeter, "Capitalism, Socialism," *Economic Policy: Readings in Political Economy*, 1961, pp. 11-113.)

e. Andrew Hacker

Hacker observes that the economy of the United States is corporation centered; two-thirds of the productive assets of the national economy is controlled by the largest 150 corporations. Hacker develops the concept of power without people. He refers to the corporation as power, the power of productive assets,

without a human constituency. The corporation has the power
to promote and defend, but its interests are more the interests of
a machine than those of the people who guide and profit from
the corporation's performance. Hacker observes that the managers
who control the corporate complexes do indeed exercise power,
but it is the vicarious power which comes from their control of
the resources of the enterprises they tend. Executives, he observes,
come and go and their terms in top positions are surprisingly
short. However the productive assets remain, continually developing new interests to be safeguarded and new demands to be
fulfilled. In the matter of who is represented as corporate power
is exercised, Hacker holds that the big corporation reflects its
power in the marketplace and in the establishment power structures. Corporations act to promote and protect organizational integrity in their own self-perpetuating interests. The phenomenon
of big corporations, managed by non-owner professional managers,
demonstrates, in Hacker's view, that corporate power through
the control of resources will be exercised in the interests of
human beings only secondarily; survival of the corporate organizational entity is the first and foremost consideration. (See Andrew
Hacker, "The Corporation and the American Future," *Challenge*,
January, 1964, pp. 15-16.)

Ecology of Economic Theory

The above indicates diverse positions of able and knowledge-
able men. On the one hand, there is widespread recognition of
big business' accomplishments; at the same time severe criticisms
express a wariness and fearful suspicion of excessive concentrations
of unbridled power. That further adaptations of theoretical im-
plication are needed to explain the nature and behavior of big
business organizations is clear. If the business community is to
become completely immersed in finding solutions to urban problems, its own interests must be shown to be concomitantly paramount yet mutual with community interests. The mutuality of
interests of business and the urban community lies at the heart of
the functioning of the enterprising economic system. In a pluralistic political-economy where big businesses (the few) are so economically powerful and so critically necessary to get the "big"
jobs done, it may be, as some argue, that a broad social conscience
is necessary to override a merely community-oriented social
consciousness.

Economic Maxims Tumble

Time (June 2, 1958) reported that two economic maxims are dead:

(1) prices are sticky and no longer adjust themselves downward with declining demand; (2) wage rates resist downward pressures stemming from an increasing unemployment and larger numbers of job seekers. In our earlier analysis and throughout our discussion of classical doctrine the usual demand structure assumed that prices are market determined rather than administered. Or if prices are administered, the traditional analysis assumes that this fact makes no real difference, that firms with market power to administer prices will at their discretion set prices at that level at which the market would have set them. Under a regime of pure and perfect competition, when prices are universally market determined, prices are completely flexible and vary as necessary to "clear the product market." But, in the regime of bigness prices as well as wages are set by an essentially political process. This is not to say that administered pricing is conterminous with monopoly. It is to say, however, that in an oligopolistic economy in which administered prices are the rule production and therefore employment become the variables, and stable markup and sticky prices are consistent with market structure and business pricing practices.

The Business Pattern

Adam Smith certainly failed to anticipate the concentrations of economic power which have developed in the private sector. Entry to the basic industries is virtually closed due to size and capital requirements alone. Price leadership is the rule rather than the exception. The type competition postulated by Adam Smith is an anathema to professional managers of large firms. Big labor also strives to broaden its power base in an expanding arena to stifle competition in labor markets. The farm block has virtually eliminated traditional competition in agricultural pursuits through legislative rewriting of the rules of the game. The quest for stability in their own particularized markets by producer groups has been notably successful and the self-interest benefits attained have been at the expense of the traditional competitive forces in the marketplace. "If each [firm] seeks his maximum profit rationally and intelligently, he will realize that where there are only a few sellers his own move has a considerable effect upon his competitors, and that this makes it idle to suppose that they will accept without retaliation the losses he forces upon them. Since the result of a cut by any one is inevitably to decrease his own profits, no one will cut, and although the sellers are independent, the equilibrium result is the same as though there were a monopolistic agreement between them." (Edward A. Chamberlin, *The Theory of Monopolistic Competition*, 5th ed., 1947, p. 48.)

It is important to note that the above line of analysis applies to an oligopolist's behavior only when he is weighing a price decrease. This would hardly apply during periods of full capacity utilization or even during periods of moderate utilization, for in such positions the direction of contemplated target pricing is on the upside and rarely downward. An implicit central theme or assumption in such an analysis provides for a growing, fully employed economy in which the economic flows are expanding. In this instance Galbraith observes: "With inflation, the demand curves of the firm and industry are moving persistently to the right. Under these circumstances there will normally be an incomplete adaptation of oligopoly prices. Prices will not be at profit-maximizing levels in any given situation, for the situation is continually changing while the adaptation is by deliberate and discreet steps. This means that at any given time there will ordinarily be a quantum of what may be called unliquidated monopoly gains in the inflationary context. The shift in demand calls for a price increase for maximization and since the adaptation is currently incomplete, prices can at any time be raised and profits thereby enhanced." ("Market Structure and Stabilization Policy," *Review of Economics and Statistics*, May, 1957, p. 127.)

Galbraith's theme is unassailable so long as aggregate demand continues to rise (economic flows are augmented). It is the tendency toward price stickiness and the increasing demand shift up and to the right that give rise to the time lag which in turn introduces the unimposed, and hence unliquidated monopoly gains.

Price Theory Implications

Marginal analysis provides a technique for appraising behavioral patterns within differing market structures. The patterns emerging are crucial in their impact on the densely populated and monetized urban environment. The material welfare differences, in terms of consumer welfare, employment, stability, and uninhibited economic flows are significant, particularly in a highly monetized environment.

a. *The Pure Competitive Model*

In the Smithian model, under conditions of pure competition, industrial production and pricing policies are governed by rules of the economic game which tended to "optimize" material welfare for consumers. Because no firm controls sufficient output to affect price in the market place, production under conditions of equilibrium is carried to that point where the additional cost of producing the last unit (marginal cost) equals the additional revenue from the sale of the last unit (marginal revenue) equals price (average revenue). For the firm this means essentially that: total revenue minus total cost equals zero, or total revenue equals total cost. Hence, in equilibrium, unit price equals unit cost. In this portrayal the classicists included in revenue and cost concepts an opportunity or relative alternative cost concept so that returns accruing to the entrepreneur were sufficient to keep him in the business. But no "profits" as such accrued.

We also in this model pattern behavior to show that consumption flows create some two-thirds of income and that what is not spent for C is saved. Thus: $Y = C + S$ and $S = Y - C$

In the classical mold, except for temporary innovatory profits, the source of investment funds for firms was individual savings. Capital funds represented the savings of the people aggregated by savings institutions and invested by risk-taking entrepreneurs which provided for growth, increased employment, and augmented economic flows. The incentive to save and invest was the interest rate in payment for savings. This required abstinence from consumption and assumed correctly a dependence for investment funds based on an almost dysfunctional inequality in the distribution of income. In theory, the classicists merely assumed that all savings flowed automatically into investment channels.

b. *The Imperfect Competitive Model*

The goal motivations, or returns on investment (profit quest), do not change under oligopoly, but the conditions of market structure do change and behavior patterns are modified. A new game emerges. Under oligopoly, firms do control sufficient output to influence supply, and therefore price. And as Chamberlin pointed out above, firms do act characteristically with considerable regard to the presumed or anticipated reaction of their few major rival competitors. To illustrate the full import of this type market structure, in about 70 percent of all American industries, five or fewer firms account for 50 percent or more of the product production and distribution in that industry.

Under conditions of oligopoly, the firm faces a downward sloping demand curve and its marginal revenue curve falls twice as rapidly from left to right as does the average revenue curve. Under these conditions optimal output is not forthcoming, for production ceases at a point where the added cost per additional unit is far below price. In this instance, the firm has a rising marginal cost schedule, a falling marginal revenue schedule with a slope twice as steep as the firm's demand schedule. Thus the firm produces to the point where the added cost per each additional unit produced (marginal cost) equals the added cost per each additional unit sold (marginal revenue). However, this point of output is such that added cost and revenue for the last unit produced and sold lies far below the average revenue or price of the product. The net result is less than optimal output, accentuated instability, less than optimal utilization of plant and facilities, and, importantly in the highly monetized urban environment, less than optimal employment. The economic flows are less than they would be under the assumptions of the more traditional market structure. Yet this comparative summation lacks credulity for it implies that society could have the best of two economic worlds if only it would try, if in some ecological way the environment of Smith's purely competitive model could be made to encompass the autonomy, the size, the knowhow stemming from basic research, and the ability to finance and implement modern technology requiring enormous investment flows. In the concepts of modern political economy such an amalgam is perhaps theoretically logical, but the name of the game would be altered as the new rules were imposed.

If we consider the thesis that the oligopolistic market structure fails to increase material welfare, as seems inherent in the pricing and production policies followed, we must concede the rational logic of such policies. Production beyond the point where MC=MR would, in the case of a rising MC curve and a falling MR curve, cause the additional cost of producing one more unit to be greater than the additional revenue obtained from selling one more unit. No professional manager, acting in the best interest of his stockholders, could abrogate this logic. Hence, production stops at this point. These are, moreover, internal firm policies and can hardly be considered as overt abuses of power. On the other hand, any such policies which fail to benefit consumer material welfare are subject to critical scrutiny within a democratic framework. At this point in the interest of political-economic ecological adaptation to a changing structure and environment, certain questions are posed. Are oligopolistic production and pricing policies which fail to optimize consumer welfare, private policies alone or is there a legitimate and growing measure of public policy interest inherent and present in the issue? Considering "big business" interests a minority in the democratic reference in numbers, if not in power bestowed by control over huge agglomerations of resources, is the economic power establishment not perhaps the tail wagging the much larger dog, the democratic society?

A sizeable measure of public interest is inexorably involved in business policy. Some economists have postulated a sort of marginal cost-pricing control as an alternative to private, autonomously administered pricing. An agency outside the industry would set a price for basic industries (perhaps 500 firms in all included under marginal-cost-pricing control). This price would be maintained regardless of sales volume. For the firm this policy would reactivate and approximate the competitive market structure. It is submitted by authoritative, recognized scholars that such a policy would tend to bring forth fuller utilization of plant capacity, fuller employment, augmented stability in the urbanized, monetized environment, and expanding economic flows. Excess or monopoly profits accruing only because of oligopolistic market structure imperfections would be eliminated. Normal competitive profits would be earned. This is a theoretical economic position of almost impeccable logic but is as yet an unpalatable rhetoric in the political economy of the United States.

c. *The Savings Function*

Savings are the key to investment flows and economic growth. In the traditional model, individual savings were paramount. Investment was entirely inward-looking and firm oriented. Growth, from the standpoint of the political-economy, was a byproduct. As an ecological process, economic theory is developed from economic facts and tends to lag behind a dynamically changing environment. The need is for a positive theory in tune with urban economic needs. Theories of the traditional mold which deal with economic phenomena of even twenty years ago are ineffective when applied to mounting urban phenomena and its complex problems.

Until the positivistic economic theory of the post-war period was enunciated by the Employment Act of 1946 and experience based on "economic growth with stability on purpose" was added to their kit of tools, economists tended to consider the corporation as just another manifestation of "economic man," subject to the same market rules, having the same motivations, and behaving the same as the mythical number of units in a competitive market lacking the power and autonomy of self-propelling economic entities.

With the advent of the new corporate centered economic organization, the corporations proved their efficiency in the production and distribution of services. Furthermore, the acquisition of market power to administer prices and to set prices above cost introduced a new facet to economic relationships in a changed environment. In simple arithmetic:

For the oligopolist: Total Revenue is greater than total cost as per established production-pricing policies. Corporate Savings equals Total Revenue minus total cost, or $S = TR - TC$.

Since 1938 accumulation of undistributed profits has become a major factor in investment and economic expansion of plant and facilities. In effect, corporate investment decisions have tended to become: (a) quite non-sensitive to short-run money and credit conditions; (b) extremely non-sensitive to the individual saver and his investment expenditures. The firms that aggregate individual savings—life insurance companies, pension funds, mutual funds, savings and loan associations—are important in institutional investment flows, but the abstinence and interest incentive motivations are largely insignificant in regard to the individual saver and his investment behavior. Now the individual saves because he is "forced" to keep up his insurance premiums, his house payment, his installment purchases, etc.

Of the capital funds invested in American industry, about sixty percent are internally generated, largely by the conglomerates. An additional twenty percent consists of bank credit most readily available to those same "giant" concerns. Only the twenty percent remaining comes from personal savings aggregated by financial institutions organized for this purpose.

TENDENCIES IN SYSTEM ECOLOGY

Political economists have not yet fully absorbed the full implications of the ecological impact on the "system" to have the large (few) corporations as the prime movers in the transposition of the savings of the economy into investment. With the market power to administer prices above costs, the "profits accruing due to market structure imperfections" take on the character of a tax on consumers. The corporate savings or undistributed profits are then transposed into economic investments. In effect, the corporate professional manager, using the power conferred upon him by the resources he commands and the imperfect market structure, in essence saves for the householders as consumers and invests such savings as are accumulated into economic growth. The householder by paying higher prices for what he buys is non-consuming what he otherwise might have consumed. So in a real sense the householder is forced to save through higher product prices just as forcibly as he pays taxes. And, the savings so accumulated are invested not in the householder's name, but in the name of the corporation. The individual saver is essentially a largely passive factor and the economic system has moved on under the impetus of ecological institutional modification to changing relationships in a changing environment. Thus in the broad general format of today's evolving economic system, the corporate power centers pattern economic investment in a manner as corporate officials direct to keep economic life abreast of society's wants and needs. Notwithstanding an almost unending listing of urban unsatisfied and unfilled needs, the political economy of the United States is moving forward soundly and progressively with expanding private investment flows combined with and building upon rigorous public investment flows in both physical and human capital.

Perspective on Business Government Relations

At the level of corporate operations executives are faced with a condition rather than a theory. The ideology of traditional "free" enterprise philosophy remains in men's minds as the way "things ought to be". Anti-government phobias still run strong. Nonetheless conditions of the times tend to push private and public objectives into closer working relationships. It is encouraging to witness that big business enterprise is turning attention to urban problems not as problems, but rather as opportunities for business, for the professions, for small businesses, and even for the individual householder.

In California, the state government put up for competitive bidding contracts for research studies intended to facilitate solution of four major problems: a rising crime rate, the need for a

data processing system for informational needs, development of
a state-wide transportation system, and waste and pollution control. The successful bidders were Aerojet-General Corporation,
Lockheed, and North American Aviation, all of which have pools
of trained scientists who could be assigned to these increasingly
complex and sophisticated problems.

BUSINESS ENTERPRISE GOALS

The large private corporation is, as we have seen, an anomaly
in regard to traditional firm theory and motivational attributes so
proscribed. Internally, the firm power structure adopts the same
pattern and hierarchy as the public corporation. For middle level
managers the motivation may best be described as budgetary
economics. The manager is judged on his ability to attain predetermined results with pre-determined resources allocated to him.
The rules of the game he plays are unilaterally passed down and
if he is to make the grade his performance is assumed within
prescribed limits. At top level, private corporate executives give
lip service to the profit motive, but hardly in the traditional concept of an anticipated residual. Targeted pricing, stabilized price mark-up procedures, and the ability to hold the
price line and profit per unit margin even in the face of falling
product demand indicate that the top level corporate executive
possesses power to manipulate within the market in order to
achieve a sufficient dividend payment and a sufficient savings for
growth investment to keep up with rival firms in the industry.
The new economic game disavows the cut-throat, the under-
handed, the frequently disastrous law of the jungle that characterized the "free" enterprising economy of only yesterday. The
goals of corporate enterprise today seem more sophisticated, more
broadly based, and more integrated in the total economic-social
fabric. These institutional characteristics may provide an important
side-effect for the urban community.

If the nature and structure of the business community is essentially as portrayed, the necessary effort to enlist business enterprise in urban development phenomena should begin in market
creation.

Space technology did not appear on its own. The know-how
and facilities were not ready and waiting when Sputnik No. 1
shook American complacency in 1957. Space technology was
created on purpose. Government scientists first determined general goals and a broad listing of needs to fill these goals. In effect,

government action created a market demand for a still undefined technology and product. Under market stimulus the necessary tools and space technology were soon pouring forth with an ever-increasing sophistication and performance quality. This is the way the enterprising system meets the needs of the times. There is no market that is not served by firms in some industry and no industry or business that does not service some market. Within the existing political-economic system technology will always be forthcoming when human needs, backed by the financial where-withall to purchase the necessary resources and knowledges, are reflected by the demand structure in some established market. Firms with resources and technical know-how are becoming increasingly involved in urban phenomena. Some large conglomerates are acting to create new markets by creating entirely new cities. At this point, it is submitted that entirely new market creating concepts are needed to enlist private enterprisers into working as partners with government at all levels to turn problems of social malaise into paying business opportunities. The economic system must be adapted to utilize the full vigor of enterprising men if physical and social decay spreading in urban places is to be halted.

.. 6 ..

The Ecological Processes
of Urban Adaptation

SINCE antiquity the urban place has formed its central economic
core around its labor market function. The role of jobs—the way
in which men prepare for, seek, and fill them—is at the very
heart of the economic system. The social-political-economic system may vary in nature and structure, but the primary economic
problems, production and distribution, are similar regardless of
institutional differences. In the Western world existing value judgments regarding social structure, the pluralistic division of power,
economic justice, equality, and opportunity to lift oneself by the
bootstraps are all related to jobs. Beyond the immediacy of the
economics of earning a living, what a man *is* becomes closely
allied with what he does. In this frame of reference, individuals
are what they know and do, their knowledge and skills become
their most exacting expression of self-identification.

TRANSITIONAL JOB ABSORPTION PATTERN

Concentration of growing masses of heterogeneous peoples into
a limited space causes frictional contacts that are more direct,
more personal, and more governing of behavioral patterns than
is the more subtle, but necessary, inter-personal cooperation required by urbanized economic and social interdependencies. The
transitional demands placed upon migrant workers who have
moved by the millions to the city are not demands related to man's
nature, but rather to his preparation, his searching out, and his
filling of increasingly complex employment requirements in the
urban environment. The transitional demands require an adjustment in the lives of workers and their families which constitutes
a major crisis economically, emotionally, and socially. Much

56

social pathology of ghetto and slum living stems from a failure to make the transition successfully from slums to job to suburbia.

In this strange, highly impersonal, and monetized urban environment, the new migrant knows the gnawing fear of economic instability. His limited financial resources are budgeted; the pressures for economic survival become paramount. Insecurities can be eliminated only as the worker, individually and in the job market, gains emotional and financial strength through employment. The transitional process through which the worker moves in his adjustment to the urban working and living environment is an important factor underlying social pathology in urban centers.

Work as a Means of Survival

Initially, the typical untrained, usually rural or small-town oriented, migrant faces the stark realities of earning money so that he may eat. His pattern of thinking and behavior is modified. He must adjust to the demands of the production line, the exactness of regularized work patterns and, importantly, the necessity of vitalizing his attention span so that he is aware and ready to cope with the job environment whether it be a matter of personal safety, accuracy, or customer service. He must learn to think of, react to, and consider his job as a distinct function removed entirely from other aspects of his daily living. He must learn to work for and with, and to be subordinate to other people without resentment or questioning. The discipline of the modern work place requires that the migrant urban worker acquire a new perspective about himself and his environment.

Work as a Social Interest

Men as social beings are inherently concerned with the self-image they present to their peers. It becomes vitally important for the worker to "get along", to "belong", to "fit in" with his fellow workers. Their lives are moulded by a conformity determined by modern technology and living and working patterns. Their symbols of status stem primarily from their work experience. As the worker gains a feeling of job security, his status drives tend to move him on toward job satisfaction stemming from pride in performance. This requires a greater job readiness, more training, the acquisition of skills, and the exercise of some independent judgment. Attitudes change from "It's a job" or "It's a living" to "I am a carpenter" or "I build machine tools" or "I drive a taxi." Identification with a job well done is a major step forward in economic performance and in adaptation to the urban environment.

The Job Family

Jobs are interrelated in functional sequence, related skills, and mutual end objectives. Job evaluation, wage and salary administration, pay differentials, training programs, and promotional sequence reflect job family or occupational patterns. Workers in this transitional phase develop identification with a broad work objective, an overall occupational goal. With this new broadly based identification workers acquire a sense of social participation, a feeling of achievement in an established work role. An inherent "internal radar" tends increasingly to polarize workers' attitudes and opinions with those of their broadly based peer groups. This in effect draws new migrants and levels of men toward each other into the labor market employment hierarchies. The closer these persons share the attitudes and opinions of the group, the less likely it is that they will think individually and independently. This is the final transitional phase in which most urban workers find their economic place in society. Identification with the broader peer group leads to the peak status position which is the goal of most urban workers. Peer group cohesiveness is clearly of growing economic and political importance in the urban environment.

The Career

It is often stated that security is an inherent something coming from within a person. Security is that feeling one has the skills, the knowledge, and the drive to succeed, to take care of one's self and family and to meet competition in frequently difficult and varied forms. In the career orientation, individuals strongly identify with work which demands a high level of competency. "I am a doctor, or lawyer, or business executive." Often their entire personalities, their self-image, and their sense of social contribution and individual fulfillment become almost indistinguishable. This transitional career phase requires exacting professional training and experience, most usually dependent upon college and post-graduate education. It has little relevance to the urban migrants who *man* the production lines and the commercial and service establishments.

THE FUNCTION OF THE SLUM

Unemployment and *no jobs* is typical of the central city slum.

Yet, the slum has historically performed an important transitional economic function for the migrating worker. Immigrants from abroad as well as from rural communities arrived in the city lacking the skills to seek and fill urban jobs. The slum provides a cheap domicile, inexpensive living, and association with other disadvantaged peers. Domestic service, sweat shops, and the most degrading of menial and brute strength tasks provide the only opportunity for the untrained. However, in the American tradition of the free enterprise system the earnest hardworking individual could rise in the open society. The development of the predominant middle class American and his subsequent movement from slum through job to vocation to suburbia is a matter of record. The American economic dream seemed clear; one's success or failure depended entirely upon his diligence, frugality, and his willingness to work. The slum constituted an enabling and transitory phase.

THE SLUM'S MATURATION AND FAILURE

At the turn of the century, the bulk of the labor force was unskilled, unlearned, and located in rural areas. Strength, not knowledge or skill, was requisite. With the coming of power, mechanics, and technological innovations, farm productivity rose higher and higher. In the post World War II era productivity gains in agriculture averaged an annual eight percent increase. The farm based labor force dropped from 60 percent in 1900 to about 5 percent in 1967. Commercial farming became mechanized and highly skill-oriented. The cotton pickers and farm hands moved to the city slums by the millions. This was to be the first transitional step.

Earlier the Poles and Irish, for example, had come to the urban place—Boston, New York, Chicago—and formed their own autonomous neighborhood communities around the church or some other old world institution relationship. The first generation struggled to sustain the culture they brought with them. Often even the mother tongue was sacrosanct, English was *verboten*. Second generation children tended to be bilingual, using the parents' native language at home and English at school and on the street. The second generation tended also to move away from the "district or neighborhood" to suburbia and integration with other indigenous middle class Americans. The third generation was all American.

In the post-war period the mobility of farm and small town migrants, particularly the Southern Negro, was accelerated. Unlike the foreign migrants, they did not tend to form tightly knit neighborhoods based on language or even on cultural consanguinities. Their common characteristics were derived for the most part from lack of education, a high proportion of illiteracy, an almost complete lack of skills, an entrenched rural psychology, and the obsequiousness expected of the Negro by the whites. Nonetheless there were Negroes who were motivated in the American tradition by free enterprise opportunity and the promise of the "open society." Many Negroes attained the job readiness requisites and acquired the competence that accompanies task and job skill status. Gradually it became apparent that the "open" society was in reality a closed society in regard to important aspects of middle class life, most importantly higher level jobs and housing.

Discrimination is estimated to cost the United States economy upwards of thirty billions of dollars in gross national product each year. Underemployment and unemployment are hard economic facts of life in Negro slums. Negro unemployment rates stand consistently at twice or more the equivalent rates of unemployed whites. Underemployment can be measured by comparing the income of whites and blacks of equal education who work at the same job level. Negro college graduates earn far less than white college graduates even when only Northern "name" university graduates are surveyed, thus leaving out arguments of the somewhat inferior standards of Southern all-Negro colleges.

In this connection, it is necessary to pinpoint the identification and magnitude of the problem. The U. S. Bureau of the Census identified some 9.7 million poor families with incomes below $3,000 in 1959. Poor families are classified in seven defined groups.*

Family Head aged 65 or older	3,002,000
Female Head aged under 65	1,557,000
Male Head of Family under age 25	614,000
Male Head of Family aged 25-64 with less than 9 years of education	3,011,000
Male Head of Family aged 25-64 who dropped out of high school	709,000

*U. S. Census of Population 1960. United States Summary.

Male Head of Family, non-white, aged
  25-64 who graduated from high school   93,000
Male Head of Family, white aged 25-64
  who graduated from high school   665,000

These figures generalize. However, of the 9.7 million poor families with yearly incomes of less than $3,000, only 665,000 were headed by white males aged 25 to 65 with twelve or more years of education. Poverty among those with a high school or above education is rare, baring special circumstances, such as physical disability. Poverty is a more natural state of economic affairs among older people, families headed by females, young men, poorly educated males, non-white persons. Not all this poverty is concentrated in urban central cities; some is rural. However, whereas rural poverty has been effectively hidden or rationalized for years in terms of alternative opportunities to survive through cultivating small garden plots, the urban massive concentrations of humanity in deliberately limited space in a highly monetized economy are becoming more and more articulate as both economic and political forces. These people can no longer be ignored; the market must include them. The slum trap can and must be eliminated through market processes. The rules of the game are the key to acceptance; a new game is emerging. Economic progress among the disadvantaged poor depends upon economic opportunity. This much is basic.

ECONOMICS OF THE SLUMS

a. *Housing*

New urban migrants face an awesome environment. Their limited financial resources must be conserved. Their needs and resources inevitably lead them to slum housing. The old mansions around the city center that once housed one prominent family are divided to accommodate many in one and two room units. In the early 1950's a study of renewal housing development in southside Chicago, based on a count of existing accommodations, estimated that some 18,000 people would need to be relocated to make way for the new development. In sheer defiance of established housing norms, the Chicago Housing Authority found over 88,000 people living in what had formerly been considered normal accommodations for about 18,000.

Multiple one room family accommodations and community use of kitchen facilities and bathrooms are still not uncommon in the urban slum. For these "rat-infested" quarters the disadvantaged

migrants pay comparatively higher rents than is the case for the
higher income classifications in much better neighborhoods. Comparative ratios are higher for non-whites in terms of family incomes
and in terms of comparable living space and facilities. Opportunities to improve housing status with equal money elsewhere are
scarce because of discriminatory practices. Pressures applied to
the free market processes are sufficient to subvert market functioning, thus providing a captive consumer group for slum housing
landlords. Seemingly omnipresent in all metropoli are growing
land use areas characterized by a large proportion of shanty towns
and decrepit tenement slums. Adding to the economic discomfiture of the disadvantaged poor are inadequate urban services, including water supply, sewage facilities, public utilities and services,
public transport, uncontrolled land use, and inattention to building repair; further discomfiture, both economic and social, stems
from excessive population densities, deficient and inadequate educational and recreational facilities, and inefficient commercial and
marketing services. The urban slum testifies to a serious failure
of the market in terms of maintaining basic human dignity and
freedom, maintaining minimum human decency standards, and
creating and sustaining a viable economic living and working
environment. The almost hopeless physical conditions of the urban
slums are creating significant pressure for "social and public"
instead of the more traditional "productive and private" investments. These investment connotations are subject matter for
current discussions of the transitional system developments by
economists, editorial pundits, and politicians. While the most degrading of the slums in many cities have been razed, the larger
portion of the task of urban renewal lies ahead. In these matters the
urban environment is endeavoring to adapt itself to meet the urgent
needs of the time. However, initiative for organizing and implementing economic activities to facilitate the adaptation from slum
tenement housing to low cost respectable housing rests primarily
with the public sector.

b. *The Commercial Trap*

Small grocery stores, clothing stores, and a multitude of
variety stores mark the slum community. Many are located in
dimly lighted basements. Many barely meet and many often fail
to pass minimum health inspections. Occasionally, one finds a
small supermarket or department store. Usually, however, item for
item when quality is accounted for and balanced, the slum dweller

is forced to pay from slightly to significantly higher prices for the same goods than does the inhabitant of suburbia or higher income neighborhoods. This is partly explained in terms of "hand-to-mouth" small lot buying and consuming patterns. Another pertinent cause of higher price, lower quality merchandising lies in the credit practices. When credit is the basis for one's next meal, the bargain is one-sided. The slum purchaser with an erratic income earning pattern stays eternally in debt to the local store. This is almost (like the mill town company store) a cultural phenomenon in the slum environment. In terms of consumer durables such as televisions, automobiles, washers, dryers, refrigerators, and package food plans the record is so tainted with fraud as to be a serious indictment of the free enterprise system. When people cannot or will not read the fine print in installment purchase agreements with some degree of understanding, they fall prey to the unscrupulous. Price hijacking, usurious interest rates, unjustified service charges, and unwarranted repossession characterize the practice of unscrupulous merchandising which further handicaps the disadvantaged poor. But, says Theodore Levitt: "The business man exists for one purpose, to create and deliver value satisfaction at a profit to himself. . . . If what is offered can be sold at a profit, then it is legitimate . . . the cultural, spiritual, and moral consequences are none of his concern." ("Are Advertising and Marketing Corrupting Society?" *Advertising Age*, October 6, 1958, p. 89.)

c. *Transportation*

Spreading slum areas present an anomalous vacuum situation in the metropolis. Economically, the area inhibits communication between the central business district and suburbia. Just a few years ago, in city after city, main arterial streets into the central city wound inevitably through abject, dilapidated slum neighborhoods. In the last decade, the freeway, expressway, parkway, multi-lane limited-access superhighways speed the driver through these areas so rapidly that the slum is almost as unnoticed as the rural shack. However, visible or not, the economic slum vacuum is there. Except for the limited-access express highways bypassing the slum neighborhood, traffic is slowed down by narrow streets, disorderly pedestrian traffic, use of streets as playgrounds, vending stands, and other obstacles. More than this the spreading slum around the CBD induces businesses to "jump" the economic vacuum to the suburban shopping center. It seems clear

that the typical motivation for entrepreneurs is not present among
the urban "low income and no income" slum domiciled families.

The obvious collateral question follows: if firms offering job
opportunities and income do not find it economically feasible to
locate in slum neighborhoods why don't slum inhabitants commute to the suburbs where plants are moving, or to the CBD,
the heart of the commercial district? Of course, many do commute.
Every day outgoing buses and commuting trains to suburbia
carry female domestic workers from low-income slums to work
and back to the city in late afternoon. This type employment is
dispersed throughout suburban neighborhoods; normally the house-
wife meets the domestic worker at the bus stop or train station
and completes the trip to work by private auto. Typically also,
domestic day workers are compensated for transportation expenses
over and above the hourly or daily rate of pay.

The transportation problem is accentuated for male workers
whose work is located in specific suburban plants frequently involving transfers of buses, etc., and often a jaunt on foot. The
wide dispersal of job opportunities for female domestic workers is
a public transportation advantage; the specific concentration of
employment for males at a precise point in geography and time
of shift change, makes reliance even upon adequate public transportation systems a difficulty for the typical male slum worker.
The trip to work and back is apt to constitute the most arduous
and boring part of the day. Also, a time allotment of two to
three hours each day for the trip (including waiting, travelling,
transfering, etc.) is quite normal. The pace is a difficult one to
maintain for the worker whose advance is slowed, if not blocked,
by discrimination. The wages are low, the pace is arduous, the
rise to the status of job or career identification is typically too
steep in its upward slope to sustain the will to work, to perform,
and to improve. Transportation problems, then, contribute to
slum neighborhood isolation. The problem of transporting thousands of persons from fairly dispersed residential areas to specific
work locations and back again in an orderly, efficient, and timely
manner is one problem not yet solved in urban places.

Unquestionably the automobile has provided the best answer
yet to this problem. The solution, however, causes problems as
serious as the basic mobility problem itself. The $1.50 an hour
worker can hardly afford to own and operate a dependable car
to start with; secondly in today's urban place where can he keep
it once he has acquired one? Further, unlike female workers, the

male worker is seldom reimbursed for travel expenses. Often in conversations with urban-based businessmen, the writer has wondered how frequently the lazy, indolent, undependable common laborer merely seems that way because his jalopy is old and tired, temperamental, and undependable. The number of old and decrepit abandoned cars picked up daily in large urban centers would support this supposition as an economic factor which affects the behavior of workers, at least to a limited degree.

It seems clear that mobility and the urban transportation system lie at both the economic and social heart of metropolitan organization. The impact is social in that transportation influences work and living patterns and relationships. Too often the social (and perhaps it is also necessary to say the psychological) aspects of the transportation system's impact on the urban place and its people are not fully recognized. Firm decisions governed by transportation (i.e., the need to move goods and people) start internally in the production process and continue as a cost factor through the entire marketing process. These decisions similarly bear on general and specific plant location, resource and market orientation, plant expansion, technological innovations and adaptations, and the commuting patterns and hence living space patterns and organization. In many ways, the nation is only beginning to sense fully the mobility problems of the immediate future. This is particularly true of growing urban places. Recognition that transportation systems have both economic and social dimensions is the first step in sound urban planning and system development.

In summary, decision-making by business firms and individual families within an urban place environment is subject to interacting and complex variables. For example, the family wage earner must consider the job-getting and the income-earning possibilities equally with commuting aspects and the relative attractiveness of neighborhood living in any of the various parts of the metropolis. Job seekers and job holders within the framework of the overall transportation system have a considerable range of housing and neighborhood choices except for the inevitable color discrimination barring Negroes from suburbia. Even here, however, the range of choices is increasing; income is perhaps the most basic factor in housing choice and quality in urban places generally. A business firm, also, within the parameters of the transportation system must consider not only the obvious matters such as rent, ease of shipping goods, and the availability of supporting

services, but also its ability to marshall an adequate labor force
to meet its needs at a competitive wage cost.

In these decision-making processes of firms and households lie
important economic and social values for our society—for philosophical as well as practical reasons. The full attainment of these
values lies in freedom of choice facilitated by information explaining available alternatives for both firms and households, assisted by
the effectiveness of the transportation system in moving people and
goods. Transportation and mobility augment urban economic alternatives with regard to housing and plant location, commuting patterns, and markets.

The Market System's Isolationism

Capitalism, as described in the classical tradition, emphasized
the individual and his freedom. Economically, such freedom means
freedom to choose one's vocation according to his bent and talents
and to expand his income to achieve maximum utility. This freedom of choice is a characteristic feature of individualism and
freedom in the economic arena.

In addition, Adam Smith interpreted the powerful personal
motivation of self-interest, or selfish pursuit in one's own self-
interest. This was contrary to the tradition of family, tribal,
manorial, and church principled concepts of group interest that
"each is his brother's keeper." However, in Smith's traditional
welfare economics, within the system parameters and the rules of
the game established, the pursuit of selfish interests by the individual maximizes the community group interest. Smith's traditional individualism inherently presupposes a self-directed quality.
The individual works and spends the income earned in independent, self-directed ways, with only his own gain and personal
well-being in mind. He does not conceive of the public good
except as it coincides, or fails to coincide, with his own private
good.

Smith measured a nation's wealth not in gold but rather in
the level of the stock of goods available for consumption. Goods
and services become in the enterprise economic system the means
to satisfaction, whether the satisfaction is measured in terms of
utility stemming from ostentatious display or the utility of direct
consumption of basic foodstuffs. In this sense the economic system
generates and depends upon an outside force motivating the individual objectively and emotionally. With goods and services, and
the power and status they bestow, linked inextricably to the

protestant ethic and to measurable and demonstrable goals of middle class culture, the market system insofar as it promoted production and employment gained the approval of economists. Events evolved, however, which tended to subvert this market oriented motivation and which are urgently signaling some political-economy system reform and modification.

THE ECONOMIC ACTIVIST

Middle class culture, i.e., the acquisitive quest for the good things in life, means progressivism for middle and upper income activist Americans. Challenged and motivated by his changing environment, he looks forward to tomorrow with some joy and anticipation. Tomorrow promises new opportunities, new experiences, a new job challenge perhaps or a new place of residence. American vocational and residential mobility substantiates the activist American's continuing quest for self-improvement of his lot. He expects and wants more for his children than he has had. With a pleasant anticipation he looks ahead to a better education, a better job, a better home, and a fuller life for his children.

The economic activist finds that ideas are central to his behavior and motivation. Something beyond and "bigger" than himself motivates his strivings and endeavors.

Economic motivations may take the form of a moral object, a principle, a material object, or perhaps a status symbol such as property ownership, income level, job skill, status in life, or perhaps an educational achievement. The market oriented economic activist as his personal achievement goals adopts those conceptual motivators which are extrinsic to his being. Everything else, economically speaking, is subordinated to economic status-seeking goals. If the neighborhood in which he lives or the company for which he works fails to provide whatever is necessary for him to achieve his goals he moves to another place where he can work toward economic goal attainment. He may also take group or other appropriate action to change the rules of the game so as to remove inhibitions to his movement forward. In any case, his behavior and the objects for which he strives can be conceptualized and defined as social and economic values. Within the parameters of the traditional free enterprise economic game, the economic activist lives in an "open door economic society" where there is the possibility of achievement beyond self, the possibility of self-development and status attainment through job, vocational and career pursuits, the possibility of self-improve-

ment through education, and the possibility of gradual climb up
the economic ladder to social recognition, status, and success.

The Economic Passivist

The economic passivist is "acted upon" in economic affairs.
The individualism he portrays is a corruption of the virtue which
underlies the economic activist's market oriented motivation. The
introspective individualistic behavior typical of a large segment
of the disadvantaged poor may prove to be a stumbling block in
our increasingly urban, technological, complex, and cooperatively
interdependent economic environment.

The economic passivist has a regressive outlook. He does not
have a pleasant economic anticipation of the future. For generations the Negro slum dweller (and poor whites also in typical
instances) has faced difficult economic and social barriers. For
him, life has been economically hard and uncertain. With little
or no education, low productivity, high unemployment and low
income, the economic passivist faces an uncertain tomorrow. In
many cases the simpler, rural life of yesterday can be recalled
nostalgically perhaps as being happier than today's ghetto existence. In so many ways while the old human relationship
values held firm, the economic passivist was regressing in the
backwash of economic change. Unable to cope with a changing
and increasingly technical environment, millions of persons faced
unemployment and abject poverty as a way of life. Concomitantly,
passive resignation tended to become the accepted economic
norm. Within the peer group of economic passivism, there was
no rebellion, little questioning, little complaining. Negro folk
music and clichés such as "blessed are the poor" reveal a fatalistic
resignation combined with religious sentiment: "If this is the way
God wants it to be, I guess this is the way it's supposed to be.
We just have to take what the Lord sends. He knows best."
While the economic activist is sure that God is most satisfied
when the individual develops and uses his God-given talents to
get ahead, the economic passivist is more prone to the belief that
God is pleased when people are satisfied with their lot.

This is not to imply that the slum dweller does not strive
at all; he does strive but not for many goals above and beyond bare object necessities. His concern is social. He seeks
recognition in his peer group. He wants to be liked, to be
accepted, to be noticed, and he will respond as a group member
to attention bestowed upon the group. Only with reluctance will

he separate himself from the peer group in which he has gained acceptance and found his status and position in life. In this social reference, the economic passivist finds his life goals in relation to other persons and is a product of group norms and behavior. While the economic activist will readily depart from a group and move out or up to achieve his economic and social goals, the economic passivist, with his strong social peer-group orientation, can find what he is seeking only through people in his associative group.

Economically, the disadvantaged passivists, live in a "closed door society," where the possibilities for economic advancement and achievement tend to be very limited. As a consequence, economic passivism (being acted upon, but not active) has led individuals to center their personal goals upon inter-personal relationships for the pursuit of some fulfillment in life. In the face of discrimination, lack of schooling, and a forbidding economic and social environment, there is probably little else that could have been done by most environmentally conditioned individuals. Only those talented and highly motivated "few" were able to move out toward the goals of the market oriented middle class culture. In this instance, it is too often overlooked that a society and economic system which tends to limit the possibilities of freely achieving object-oriented goals for all inevitably causes individuals and homogeneous groups to turn inward in search of the rewards of self-fulfillment in life.

An Economic Juxtaposition

Economic activists observe continually that the individual we have dubbed the economic passivist has no goals, is too lazy to make something of himself, and is concerned only with sensual pleasures of the moment. On the other side, the economic passivist, looking back and reflecting over the inequities of a long past history, considers the economic activist a heartless and calculating manipulator seeking his own personal gain notwithstanding damage rendered to others. The middle ground of economic juxtaposition is emerging gradually in today's urban economic environment.

Economic activist individuals also have close personal relations with others and develop ties of lasting friendship. Although these ties are more deliberately sought and cemented, enjoyment of life is found in the achievement of social as well as economic status and achievement goals. Personal relationships and group participation which renders to the activist these same important human needs of recognition and belonging provide a means for achieving extrinsic, rational goals and status fulfillment. A difference lies in the recognition by the activist that his individuality and status ties are not dependent upon a particular peer group. He can make equally meaningful new friendships as he moves along and up the economic ladder.

In contrast, the economic passivist hesitates to rock the boat in any way which might negate relationships with his peer group. Even if a job proves steady and income more certain, it is unusual to find evidence of improved economic condition in his household, his furniture, or cultural or educational outlets for himself or family. He remains content with just meeting those group goals common to his peers. He seldom looks up or beyond his peer group. He is frequently unable to articulate his personal goals, and is reluctant to discuss his future plans, prospects, or hopes.

These group orientations and ties place severe limitations upon the economic passivist who is encouraged under some current government and foundation sponsored programs to adopt an economic activist role as an entrepreneur in the business market. Due to his reference group mentality and the service orientation to his peer group, urban business opportunities for which he may qualify or train create psychological blocks, for the economic passivist finds it difficult to adapt himself to market pricing processes. Undercharging and over-extension of credit are likely to be the rule in order to preserve his reference group compatibility. Business practices governed by personal feelings to further a good fellowship relation will always be inferior to market governed business practice.

Typically in the slum ghetto, one who is businesslike is suspect. The economic passivist finds it most difficult to deal personally with persons in his peer group who fail to pay their bills or who, through past failures, beat him out of money. Such principles and moral concepts as honesty, fairness, equality, justice, and charity, he relates to group inter-personal interactions. He expects the same interpretation and behavior in relation to extrinsic, object-oriented economic business behavior and most often fails to receive it. In the economic game, conformity to the same moral interrelationship code is not the pattern. The resulting business failure then tends to make the individual reject the economic system as basically evil. In this rejection he also finds himself rejecting education, training for a better job, the profit motive, the economic system, and the social structure in toto. It is little wonder that the typical successful small business in the Negro ghetto is white owned and operated. The cultural background providing an intrinsic market orientation for participation in a free enterprising system has been lacking among Negroes generally. Their participation and entrance into the economic mainstream will require more than merely job training. A philosophical and cultural interchange must occur also.

It is interesting, however, to watch the in-roads television has made in the last ten years. TV is the very symbol of the outside world and marks nearly every aspect of market-oriented middle class values, brunting the effectiveness of the passive economic individual's goals and motivations. The constant drumming of most effective advertising and the promotion of objects and status symbols into every ear and flashing them in every eye has done much to change the ideas of the public in regard to human relationships and business behavior. The "demonstration" effect of TV advertising and affluence in the city as observed by even the most casual viewing slum dweller is unquestionably underpinning much motivation in the frequently misnomered race riots. In the opinion of many, racial issues are merely an excuse for economic pillaging and plundering by the have nots against the haves. The Negro leader's sensitivity to and capture of the peer group, and not merely independent Negroes gathered together for a momentary common cause, is of tremendous significance. Behind the scene lie basic economic issues the system must come to encompass. The cure, however, is cultural and social as well as economic.

.. 7 ..

Toward a Theory of Urban
Political Economy

POLITICAL-ECONOMY "basics" embedded in principles articulated by John Locke and Adam Smith provided guidelines for the early leaders of our nation. Representative government and a free market economy provided a framework for the free enterprising system. Traditionally, the system provided for individual decision-making based on self interest and rational choice. With rather severe qualifications, the philosophy held despite imperfections of environmental economic realities.

After observing and cataloguing ecological patterns of a changing economic game, is it possible to write a new economic theory encompassing a body of knowledge and principles sufficiently autonomous that we can call it a theory of urban political economy? Can an autonomous, self-contained economic theory be posited (normative and positive) that encompasses a "service" oriented economic functioning within an urban mixture of individual and collective—public and private—decision-making entities?

THE ECONOMIC SYSTEM "SERVICES"

An economic service connotation is used to posit the economic system to be a set of rules subject to change. The market is recognized as an institution created by man to facilitate the playing of the economic game according to established, but flexible, rules (constraints and proscriptions). Principally, the economic system "services" society through (1) producing those goods and services society wants, (2) creating and distributing income, and (3) providing for economic growth and expansion. Since 1900, particularly, American society has attained an autonomous self-identification and an internal structure of pluralistic and organized sub-cultures

72

which subscribe to the goals defined and endorsed by our middle class value system. To meet the needs of a mature purposive-minded society economic activities have also achieved an heretofore unattainable stance of economic organization and structuring of economic power.

In the twentieth century and most markedly in the period since World War II, the political economy has experienced dynamic change. The political economy has had the task of servicing a rapidly growing population with a changing age distribution, and adapting to a biological revolution which has extended longevity, with a subsequent emergence of old-age groups organizing and pressing for political-economic actions in their favor as retired life styles are modified and revised toward more affluence. In this century the political economy has had to service the nation as it fought two major world wars, two undeclared "police" actions in the Far East thousands of miles from our shores, competed in a cold war and a space race, suffered the deepest and longest depression in its history, and enjoyed the greatest surge of affluence ever experienced by man. The nation has also experienced industrializing-urbanizing trends revolutionizing the way people work and live; life styles are unrecognizable from even a single generation ago. The ideas of "making a living" through efforts of a self-sufficing family effort are gone with yesteryear. Today, no urban family can "make" a living, instead, the urban worker "earns" a living in obtaining that income necessary to sustain himself and family in the highly monetized environment of the urban place. The growing mutual interdependencies of human activities in a highly monetized urban environment requires a broader based, more efficient political-economy servicing.

SIGNS OF SYSTEM CHANGE

In an urban environment favoring a libertarian philosophy men readily exercise their liberty of thought and advocate full civil liberties for all. Economically, the urban place has become the mecca for small business enterprises which, while seeking compensation for their endeavors, are seeking assistance from all levels of governments thus exhibiting their inability to remain "independent" in a changing market structure centralizing economic power. In both an economic and social frame, urban dwellers seek "to belong" through collective organization and group status, thus relinquishing or abridging their power of entering into individual contracts and of rendering individual protest or purposive philanthropic action. Rather than bargain individually or act independently, socially, or economically, urbanites look to collective membership in organizations. In so doing, they surrender the power of individual contract and action for the status they gain as members. These organizations "bargain and decide collectively" for their members and set forth the rules governing behavior within the group. We see this in trade unions, professional and educational associations, philanthropic aid societies, and religious entities. Similarly, public agencies do "things" which service the urban group collectively. Likewise, in the private sector corporations act to acquire, use, and dispose of property, to enter into contracts, and to otherwise manage corporate affairs in the "collective" interests of owner shareholders. To recognize the political-economy for what it is and does in servicing a sophisticated, increasingly autonomous urban society, the complex economic system is coordinated by the need to weld together into a single functioning autonomous economic organism the different stresses and strains of a growing and diversified urban community.

THE URBAN ECONOMIC BASE

Economics is a study of choice as exemplified by human behavior within the parameters of established rules governing play of the economic game. With rapid and extensive industrialization and urbanization, choice in the allocation, utilization, and development of resources and production processes becomes a sophisticated and complex process. The methodology and technology of change and choice alike are being modified.

In the context of an urban base resource "mix", political-economy activities supporting urban economic system functioning may be classified generally as:

1. Primary Processes:
    a. Production: agriculture, agri-business, manufacturing, processing, assembly;
    b. Distribution: warehousing, transporting, marketing, communicating.
2. General Business Service Processes:
    a. Financial Institutions to service business, governments, and individuals;
    b. Insurance Institutions to service the community;
    c. Educational institutions to service business needs, to service government needs, and to provide the means for

      individual development of requisite job skills and knowl-
edges (both public and private institutions);

  d. Advisory services, including business and government
consulting advisory services, engineering, scientific, etc.

3. Public Services:

  a. Public over-head capital support bases to service business,
householder, and community needs as to land accessibility and use, transportation systems, power, communication, public health facilities, and necessary related urban government service functions;

  b. Protection of life and property;

  c. Recreation and Park facilities;

  d. Education facilities (at all levels);

  e. Cultural facilities and outlets.

Comparative Economic Advantage

More and more, as the urbanizing-industrializing development
trends concentrate population and economic activity, regional
economic competition becomes competition between urban place
centers. In a complex political economy, economic opportunities
are constantly springing up in one urban place and disappearing
in another. Fundamental differences in the economic advantages
of regional and urban places draw people and economic activity
from one urban place into another. Factors that shift the location
of economic activity from one urban place to another, technological
innovations, changing size of markets, exhaustion of resources,
shifts in tastes and markets, and changes in technology and/or
organization are practically beyond local control, especially over
short time spans.

    Urban communities do, however, have a choice in influencing
factors that guide the processes of economic adjustment. Such
processes reflect time lags, failures to locate areas of opportunity
for economic activity, inability to diagnose reasons for success
or failure of businesses, and difficulties in developing the new
urban oriented resources and competing with other urban regional
centers for economic producers. Also, in each urban center
economic adjustment calls forth differing mixes of basic industrial
firms, commercial and service activities, and allied public functional
services. The differing urban regional center incidence of innovators
and innovations is subject to significant influence by the presence
of new urban oriented resources.

Developing New Urban Oriented Resources

Power

The urban community must provide for (1) production and distribution of power through direct municipal action, or (2) cooperate with a private power utility in providing rights-of-way for producing and distributing electric, gas, or other type power to service the business sector, the householders, and the public sector. Without exception, power to run the economic machine is a key urban resource.

Natural Resources

When considering natural resources, urban complexes (more in the past than now) were oriented toward such resources as coal, limestone, ore, or timber. These natural resources are relatively scarce in relation to demands for them, and their relative scarcity and utility established for them an exchange value in the market place. Further, the relativity of economic scarcity of natural resources varies not only with demand, but also with the technology available for efficient exploitation within broad parameters of resource conservation and the availability or feasibility of developing acceptable substitutes. (See Hans H. Landsberg, *Natural Resources for U. S. Growth: A Look Ahead to the Year 2000*, 1964.)

Industrialization-urbanization has brought about the need for economic adjustment. In the traditional economic game of "making a living" of rural yesteryear, arable land with an ample supply of water was the important resource. In recent years a whole new set of resources became important. Technology and the control of capital became the key to the control and exercise of economic power through market processes. Technology freed production more and more from its dependence upon natural resources. Other factors came into strong consideration for site selection. Among these were the natural amenity resources: year-round climate, accessibility to the sea-shore and/or mountains for recreation, and a pleasant natural environment generally. Man-made amenity resources contributing to desirable urban environments also became important considerations in site selection. In many instances urban growth has monetized what in less populated communities were free goods and effectively converted them into economic goods.

Urban Land

Urban land values have sky-rocketed as rapid urbanization contributed to its relative scarcity. Henry George recognized this principle as a basis for his single-tax; he noted that the growth of population in urban centers creates a scarcity of land and causes values to rise. This results in a greater tax income for the local government which can be used for the common good and development of the community. In George's philosophy, society, not the individual owner, created the increased land value and society should reap the benefits of its own actions to further improve and enhance the urban environment through local government support.

The realities of urban land use, its special qualities, and the demands made upon it may trigger changes in viewpoints regarding it as a resource. Demands for spatial differentiation in allocation and use evolve as each urban complex acquires its unique characteristic patterns in adjusting to production site demands, market accessibility, and the urban center's particular "mix" of economic activities.

Urban land use, in spite of its crucial economic importance as a resource, is inexplicably disorganized and haphazard. We recognize, in planning for urban land use, that two dimensional planning is outdated and inadequate. Three dimensional land use including "sky space" is essential. High rise office buildings, high rise apartment buildings, multi-story stores and parking garages are evident in all metropolitan centers and are necessary to reduce unit land space costs. Yet, even the most casual observer notes in urban centers a preponderance of under-utilized land space, one story, often decrepit buildings, empty space being used for parking lots or sometimes unused. Owners are candidly holding property and awaiting developments which will further appreciate property values and awaiting also that developer willing to pay their inflated price. Insofar as the price-mechanism working within the market framework contributes to under-utilization of the scarce urban land resource, community environmental development and improvement is delayed. Neither economic theory nor economic practice in the marketplace, however, tells us how much of the scarce urban land resource should be used for streets, or expressways, or for the parking of cars, or really for any specific use. How much are streets worth to the city—underground, surface, and raised?

Demands for land space in and near large urban centers create market and marketing problems which tax the ingenuity, energies, and intellectual resourcefulness of the local business community, government administrators, and individual property owners and developers. Solutions to land use and spatial distribution problems must be examined with long-run optimal solutions in mind.

Pure Water

Fresh water becomes an economic resource in the urban place.
Even thirty years ago, economists could argue that water was
a free good provided by nature. The water bill paid by the householder and firm each month was payment for the piping and
pumping services required to create time and place utility by transporting the water from the spring, the river, or the lake to the
householder or firm user. Clean water for consumption, for
recreation, and for aesthetic value is becoming a scarce and vital
urban oriented resource. The impact of water pollution on fish
and plant life in and along our rivers and along our ocean shores is
under current intensive study with dire predictions anticipated.
The economic ecological effects of water pollution on urban life
and work is not yet known, but that the problem is critical is
accepted as given datum. Fresh pure water is an increasingly
important urban oriented resource crucial to urban environmental
development.

Pure Air

Air, perhaps the most abundant and pervasive of all free goods,
is becoming an economic good in urban places. To improve livability in hot humid climates, technology development gave us
refrigerated "cool" air. Cool air, then, became an economic good.
Likewise, as technology enabled man to fly in the high thin
atmosphere, air had to be "canned" in pressurized cabins with
canned oxygen available in event of emergency. Application of
technology to air conditioning moved air into the economic arena.

Air pollution, in Los Angeles particularly (although such pollution from autos, smoke stacks, garbage incinerators, coal furnaces,
etc., are present in all urban centers), has provoked national concern
over pollution of air. The incidence of respiratory disease, em-
physema, chronic bronchitis, and related diseases has increased
directly as air pollution has become more intense and widespread.
Actions to reduce and control air polluters are being invoked, although slowly because the economic cost is high. Clean air is a
national as well as an urban resource. Its conservation is an economic
"must."

Human Resources

Adam Smith saw specialization, particularly of labor, as the
cause of the wealth of nations. The urban industrial-business
complex allows and requires a specialization of human knowledges
and skills unprecedented in history. A measure of urban size is

reflected in a perusal of the medical specialties in the yellow pages of the telephone book. It is quite easy to judge the relative size of the urban place by noting medical specialties present. Similarly, specialization within the legal profession, financial services, engineering and mechanical trades, stores, shops, and many other areas characterize the city size.

Urban areas provide the best in institutional support and quality for investment in human capital. Individuals with exceptional minds and the recipients of sound educational investment may be a far greater asset to an urban political-economy than natural resource orientation or a natural port facility. Men with brains and initiative create new ideas, new processes and products, and eventually new firms and industries. The pulling power of brainpower in urban economic development is clearly acceptable as a developable urban resource. Growth of an urban economy, its viability, and its ability to develop an attractive, healthy, and functional environment are increasingly tied to a brainpower base and progressive leadership. For the nation, the President's Council of Economic Advisors suggests that continued high levels of economic activity depend upon maintaining a high level of investment, a high level of basic and applied research, and a high level of education. The same counsel applies with equal strength to the metropolitan complex. Education and the level of skills and knowledges present a key urban oriented resource.

Man-Made Environmental Amenities

Efforts to reclaim, rehabilitate, and revitalize areas of urban places that have been allowed to deteriorate into dysfunctional economic "slum" sections emphasize two basic urban economic principles:

1. organization of the political economy in the urban center for economic activity is a primary function and responsibility of the public sector, and
2. the flow of public social-capital overhead investment funds must necessarily precede the flow of private development investment funds.

Ecologically, the processes of adjustment to the urban environment and the structuring of the environment itself are first and foremost the responsibility of the public sector. Concomitantly, although governments, and particularly local governments, do produce some "thing-products" as well as condition the environment, society uses private business enterprise as the means "for getting things done."

Man-made environmental amenities comprise essentially the functions performed and services provided by the local public sector plus private enterprise developments built on the basic economic social-capital foundation and within the environment structured by the public sector. It is in the public sector at the local level where the rules governing economic behavior are written. Clearly, local governments are direct participative partners with business enterprise in the economic production processes. Local governments are expected to have the proper facilities and environment "in place" as a prerequisite before firm executives can be expected to select a given urban entity for an expanded or new business enterprise. This means (1) a progressive local government administration, (2) organization and availability of industrial park sites, (3) adequate zoning regulations, (4) a free flowing transportation network so as to assure easy site accessibility, (5) a well-supported, progressive and quality educational system at all levels, (6) attractive and well serviced neighborhoods where housing, parks, and recreational facilities are available, (7) good clean water for consumption and production uses, (8) adequate public health facilities including hospitals, industrial sewerage, storm sewers, solid waste collection and garbage incineration, (9) cultural facilities including museums, zoos, auditoriums, art centers, a community theater and symphony, a sports arena, etc. There seems no precise theoretical or empirically determined end to functions performed by municipal governments in metropolitan centers.

A theory of urban economics must include the proposition that the primary role of regional political-economic organization and environmental conditioning rests with the public sector. The decisions made by public officials are based directly upon economic functioning, the economizing of resources, the utilization of resources in varying production mixes, the balance and direction of economic development, and importantly upon the level of employment and income that is generated through economic activities. In building a theory of urban economics, the structure must necessarily include political as well as economic factors.

Property Rights

Our perspective of the economic game assumes that the system of "mixed" capitalism rests on two fundamental institutions: (1) private property, and (2) freedom of contract. In simpler environmental systems these institutional concepts were clear-cut and unquestioned. Property rights comprised a social instrument designed to establish relationships and behavior patterns, and they formed the basis for expectations one could hold in regard to the behavior of others.

As technology increased *man's* ability to tap natural resources, to denude wide areas of timber, to destroy rapaciously the fertility of the soil, to breathe pollution into the air through belching smokestacks, and to pollute streams and ocean shores to the point of an ecological disaster, the problems of externalities stemming from private acquisition, use, and disposal of property moved to the forefront for political-economic system consideration. Economic ecological considerations as they affect private property and freedom of contract are at the theoretical apex of the environmental flux in metropolitan urban complexes. In biological terms, ecology is defined as "the study of the relation of organisms or groups of organisms to their environment, or the science of the interrelations between living organisms and their environment." (See Eugene P. Odum, *Fundamentals of Ecology*, 1953, p. 3.) A study of economic human ecology suggests that as adjustment to the urban environment proceeds, the rules of the game relating to property change. External aspects of individual behaviorial patterns gain economic, political, and social significance.

Dr. Allan Gregg, director emeritus of the medical division of the Rockefeller Foundation, illustrates externality with his query: "Is man a biological cancer? There is an alarming parallel between the growth of a cancer in the body of an organism and the growth of human population in the earth's ecological economy. If this idea is valid, and if man is indeed hurrying off to such a macabre 'submit,' humanity should now face the question of an optimum population, not only in terms of politics and economics, but in terms of a more healthy relationship between the human species and other forms of life on the planet earth." (See A. Gregg, "Hidden Hunger at the Summit," *Population Bulletin*, Vol. II, August, 1955, p. 74, Rockefeller Foundation.) Dr. A. J. Carlson puts the problem in more earthy language: "If we breed like rabbits, in the long run we have to live and die like rabbits." ("Science Versus Life," *Journal of the American Medical Association*, Vol. 157, April 16, 1955, p. 1440.) Certainly the Malthusian pessimism suggested by the dire speculations on the current world-wide population explosion illustrates vividly the external effects of individually determined reproduction and population growth rates. The simile applies equally to uncontrolled haphazard population growth and life styles in densely packed urban environments.

Returning to property rights, society grants the owner of property that "right" to act in given ways and society protects the owner in that right. Inherent in property rights is the right and ability through use of property to benefit oneself (internality) and/or to harm or benefit others (externality). For example, a private enterprising firm may harm a competing firm through producing a new or better product or service (an internality for the successful firm, an externality for the other). However, one firm entrepreneur may not eliminate a competitor by "gunning him down." At the same time an owner of property may be legally within his rights to shoot an intruder, but the rules of the game may be so prescribed as to prohibit reducing his prices below a price floor or holding fire sales or "going out of business" sales. Externalities also benefit others. A newly established firm in the community providing basic jobs and new and larger income flows improves the economic environment for the retailer, the doctor, the builder-developer, and others. At the same time if the new firm belches smoke and fetid odors, or pollutes the water, adverse externalities are imposed on the community.

It is theoretically sound to consider that a primary social objective of granting corporate and individual property "rights" is to provide incentive to optimize internalization in the allocation and use of property. Efficient utilization of resources at one's control reflects the maximization of internalities in the search for revenues over costs. Economic organization patterns and the oligopolistic character of the American business community ascertain the efforts of firms to gain control over externalities by making them controllable internalities. The effect has been more efficient production, less uncertainty in business decisionmaking, improved investment flows and productivity, and an improved cost-benefit relation supporting profit margins. At the same time if we look beyond the firm to the urban political-economy, it becomes obvious that every private cost-benefit associated with community social inter-dependencies is a potential externality, either favorable or unfavorable to the total urban environment. A theory of political economy for urban places must include ideas that minimize individual and firm internalities which are disadvantageous to the urban environment. Individual property "rights" are conferred by society and should not be used for individual benefits at the cost of obvious disadvantages to society. A major modification of

the rules of the game may well impinge upon the free enterprising system if government finds it necessary to control and
prohibit such disadvantageous externalities as air and water pollution and related private actions which prove deleterious to the
urban environment.

A Shift to the Rights of Persons

Ecological shifts from the traditional emphasis upon the rights
and protection of property to an increasing recognition of the
rights of persons are evident on every hand in urbanizing centers.
Over and above those national goals which assure equality of justice
and opportunity, there emerges a broader conception of the
equality of human needs, not only for health and minimum standards
of living but also for the dignity and integrity of the individual.
Expressions of this shift in emphasis can be observed on every
hand in fair employment practices, joint negotiation in economic
matters related to work, and consumption of jointly provided
public facilities, school integration, integration of publicly provided facilities and public facilities operated by private enterprise
(buses, trains, motels, hotels, restaurants, etc.). For the most
part the change in emphasis and individual expectations are fos-
tered by governmental actions at all levels, particularly the local
urban level where government directly touches the lives of all
citizens. Creative federalism now provides a wide range of professional and technical assistance and financial support at the
local level in the political economy.

The highly monetized urban environment characterized by
extreme specialization and sensitive interacting economic interdependencies opens new vistas of social responsibility and obligation. Today hardly anyone openly argues any longer that individual freedom means freedom for only some people to do certain
things. Now, the demand is for freedom in general, freedom as
a matter of principle, freedom for all. Once freedom is extended
from that limited class which could take economic well-being
through status and hierarchy for granted to the common people
who are concerned primarily with their daily bread and rent,
freedom from the economic constraint of want is clearly as crucial
an issue as our forefathers considered their freedom from the
political restraint of kings and dictators. In the urban economic
environment with its constraints on alternative opportunities, freedom if it means anything at all must include freedom from want.

Certainly this concept is inherent in the current welfare system, old age and survivors insurance, unemployment compensation, both public and private retirement programs for lay employees, and medicare. Certainly the idea that links unemployment and poverty is implicit in the Employment Act of 1946. In substance this philosophy focuses upon a great American dichotomy. Every American citizen has a right to a decent minimal standard of living; but *earnings not subsidies or welfare should be the primary source of income for those who are able and of working age.* This dichotomy reflects the familiar and universally held market based doctrines expounded in public policy as interpreted by the writer:

1. society, through its political economy, has an obligation to assure a decent minimal standard of well-being for all its members in its own self-interest if social and economic relationships are to remain stable and orderly (a requisite to insure the domestic tranquility and to promote the common welfare);

2. society, through its political economy, has an obligation to assure useful and productive work opportunities for all members of society within their capacity to perform (to provide equal justice and equal opportunity for all);

3. society, through its political economy, has the obligation and the right to see to it that work is performed (to ascertain the facility and functioning of the market mechanism).

The attention now given generally to job opportunities by maintaining a vibrant, growing economy stems from the breakdown in the 1930's of the traditional economic wisdom. The Employment Act of 1946 obligates the Federal Government to use its full powers to sustain those conditions conducive to full employment. However, any theory of urban political economy must recognize that the "new" poor of 1969 are the product of an economic environment far removed from that of the 1930's.

Migration of millions of largely uneducated, unskilled, and unemployed persons to urban places is a new phenomenon of our times, at least in its magnitude. Accompanying this shift to the urban place have been the sharpest, most rapid, and most dramatic technological changes ever experienced in labor market requirements. Many of these millions of urban migrants were or have become untrainable and technologically unemployable in the complex, technical environment of modern, urban-based economic market activity. Despite the unprecedented rise in gross national product from $419 billion in 1956 to $740 billion in 1966 and a rise in the civilian labor force from 67 million to 77 million, welfare roles expanded from 5.8 million to 8 million persons and direct welfare costs rose from $3 billion to $6.5 billion.

Welfare as presently administered to the poverty stricken has a perverse effect on (1) the motivational incentive of the poor to find jobs in the labor market so as to work their way off the dole, and (2) on the incentives to hold families together. The rules for change are under consideration in the Congress, but the rule has been essentially a 100% tax on dollars earned, that is for every dollar a welfare recipient earns, a dollar is deducted from his welfare check. The incentive to work is blunted by this negative financial practice.

Remedies most frequently encountered for attacking the poverty syndrome are:

1. aid all the poor, all 32 million existing below the minimum poverty income level as defined by government, and

2. provide the necessary training facilities for skill acquisition; then, let the economic pressures of the market take their natural course.

However, it would be prudent to consider that the national welfare roles are not filled to overflowing with able-bodied men. There are now receiving aid a million mothers with dependent children who could probably work outside the home if day-care for children were available at rates they could afford. In regard to the frequently voiced intention to "get tough," welfare administrators have been so determined and successful at keeping able-bodied men off the welfare roles that critics have accused the system of encouraging the break-up of poor families.

THE MINIMUM INCOME PROPOSAL

As we view the problems of poverty and welfare it seems reasonable to replace the built-in lack of incentive to work with positive market incentives. A positive theory of urban political economy must encompass the market aspect of economic motivation. Proposals for family allowances or negative income taxes must be studied as measures advocating purposive action to restore people disadvantaged by the rapidity of change to the mainstream of economic and social affairs. The aim must be to attack poverty, not to institutionalize it.

In this reference, Lady Juliette Evangeline Rhys-Williams, the mother of transfer-of-income-by-taxation plans, proposed in 1943 that a "social dividend" be paid to every man, woman, and child in the British Isles. All welfare services should be combined into a single comprehensive system that would give stipends to all, not just those in need. (See Christopher Green, "Guaranteed Income Plans—Which One is Best?", *Transaction*, Jan.-Feb., 1968.)

Lady Rhys-Williams' idea grew out of her discontent with unemployment insurance which, she felt, tended to reduce market incentives to accept jobs. In *Something to Look Forward To*, she wrote, "The Lion in the path of curing want by means of social insurance is the fact that if the standard of unemployment pay is raised to a level that real want is banished, then the advantages of working for wages largely disappears."

As a solution, she advocated the abandonment of the existing social-insurance system and its philosophy that the state help only the destitute and the sick. Her new philosophy rests upon "the democratic principle that the state owes precisely the same benefits to every one of its citizens." However, she recommended that any able-bodied man who refused to work be denied benefits. Thus Lady Rhys-Williams combined legal and economic pressures to encourage the "right" decision, the decision to work. C. E. Ayres, who advocated the same principle in 1962 (see his *The Industrial Economy*), would have every member of the community receive a basic independent income, the same for all, and just sufficient to cover the minimum of subsistence. Ayres observed that all taxpayers already benefit from a subsidy—exemptions for dependents—and that it is only a step from tax deductions to direct payment.

Social dividends to all families, rich or poor, could fill the entire poverty gap between the established minimal decency income level and actual earnings. The negative income tax proposal would close only a portion of the gap and would benefit the poor exclusively. Government would make payments based on negative rates to people whose earnings fell below the established poverty line.

While eschewing details, the several guaranteed income proposals expounded are similar in their essentials:

a. their aim is to supplement the anti-poverty programs;

b. emphasis is upon family income as the eligibility determinant rather than age, physical disability, dependent children, and the like;

c. all make use of the transfer of income-by-taxation as the vehicle for redistributing income.

Now to squarely face the issue: Is there an economic justification to support minimum income proposals?

Between 1960 and 1966 (five years of dynamic change) national income *in real terms* increased by ⅓. Output per man hour increased by 23 percent. Productivity improvements were due to increased investment flows into new technology and improved management and training and education of employees, i.e., investment in human capital. This rapid improvement in the standard of living, however, brought with it new and difficult problems. The "new" poor could no longer exercise a decision to work. Trapped in ghetto poverty, these hard core unemployed failed to benefit by economic improvements. In addition, some 6 percent of all American families headed by a fully employed male worker were below the poverty line in 1960. This employed group is about 26 percent of all poor families. Another group—15 percent of all poor families—is headed by a chronically unemployed man or by one who works only part-time. The aged, the family consisting of a female head with children, and the disabled are increasingly becoming the dominant groups of "hard-core poor", accounting for about one-half of all poor families. For this group, rapid economic growth in the urban marketplace and full employment can do little to solve their problems. For them, cash benefits are essential to maintain a semblance of individual freedom and human dignity. Where children are involved, cash benefits and minimal living standards may be the key to opening the door for escape from the second-generation poverty trap. This minimal investment in youthful human capital can be expected to pay extra economic dividends to coming generations.

For those who can work, economic growth and full employment can work toward reducing poverty. For those displaced by rapid technological change, minimal income cash benefits can alleviate the immediate rigors of poverty while the unemployed worker relocates with another employer, or while he acquires new skills through training to upgrade his sale-ability in the labor market. Freedom is enhanced and human dignity is preserved.

In December 1967, Secretary of Labor Wirtz reported that the unemployment rate for non-whites was over double the white rate. Further, Wirtz reported that in the large metropolitan centers where unemployment is concentrated 15 metropolitan areas accounted for 40 percent of non-white unemployment. The non-white jobless rate in the Los Angeles metropolis was 9.1 percent. In San Francisco-Oakland the rate was 9.8 percent. White unemployment in Chicago was 2.8 percent with 8.5 percent for the non-white civilian labor force; Baltimore, 2.3 to 8.2; St. Louis, 3.1 to 12.7; Newark, 3.8 to 10.5

These urban slum dwellers constitute the "new" poor. These unskilled, unemployed or underemployed, and frequently illiterate persons are the last hired, first fired, and first to be automated out of the labor market.

It seems clearly apparent that the elimination of abject poverty, from which stem so many other social ills, could bring about dramatic improvement in the general health of our urban society.

SOCIETY NEEDS TO INVEST IN PEOPLE

Continued success of our political-economic system depends not merely on the prevention of famine or the maintenance of minimal standards of living but rather on investment in people and the quality and diversity of the urban working and living environment. Just as important as physical requirements for maintaining human life is an environment in which it is possible to satisfy the requirements for human dignity, quiet, privacy, equality of opportunity, initiative, individualism, and social mobility. These are not palliatives to urban overcrowding that produces psychotic behavior, but instead constitute very real psychological and physiological necessities. Just as the nation makes an economic investment in youth and assures each person a basic education, an equally beneficial economic investment should be made to assure children minimal standards of food, health, housing, clothing, and recreation. With new skill and knowledge and increased motivation the "right" decisions to work will deliver economic dividends.

A minimum income plan as an investment in human capital seems a step in the right economic direction, consistent with national objectives in a changed and changing urban environment. A workable plan of minimum income maintenance should contain these three essential provisions: *First*, it should preserve positive incentives to work for those able to get jobs and to increase their earnings above the minimal base; *Second*, it should be efficient in the sense of filling the poverty gap for all, without favoring some and ignoring others; and *Third*, it should be relatively simple to administer.

A free society which invokes pervasive democratic processes in urban centers, needs the guidance of basic principles congruent with the requirements and opportunities encompassed in the new urban environment. We can look for guidance to the national goals enunciated in the Preamble to the Constitution and to the American value system. A theory of urban political economy will need to rationalize departures from the persistence of anachronistic beliefs, practices, and rules of the economic game. The aggressive positivism being exercised in political activity at local as well as national levels of government casts new light on democratic processes and what role governments, labor unions, and businesses should play in an urbanized-industrialized pluralistic society.

. . 8 . .

Preface for Urban Problem Analysis

The theory of the city somehow cannot account for what every journalist, poet, and novelist knows—the city is a living thing. As a system of life, the city penetrates the structure of biological evolution itself, creating new urban-insect and urban-animal forms. There are urban-insects like the silver fish, carpet beetle, bedbug, and the cockroach—as special to the city as the proletariat, as urban as the bureaucrat. The rat and the alley cat are animal denizens of the city with an outlook as urban as detachment and sophisticated cynicism. The city has its representatives from the feathered world in the sparrow, the starling, and the pigeon—dodging traffic with the same *sang froid* as the rest of the urbanites, disputing in the squares and holding council in the eaves—winning a livelihood from the by-products of commerce. There are moments in every city dawn when the circles, rectangles, polygons, and triangles—the geometry of the city— seem to float in the mist, like the essence of the human spirit emancipated from the earth. There are times, on starlit nights, when its towers and spires ram upward as if to tear the darkness loose from its riveting stars and the city seems to be a strident assertion of mankind against time itself. ("Prefatory Remarks: The Theory of the City," by Don Martindale in the translation of *The City*, Max Weber, 1958, p. 10.)

Martindale wonders what is wrong and deficient about so many of the urban books now being published. Certainly it is not their statistics. Urban base studies by economists, sociologists, urban geographers, etc., are ably and competently compiled. But statistics are statistics, and for most cities are untidy statements of applied mathematics.

Martindale elaborates: "Nor can one say the urban books are deficient in the kind of items they include. What is a city without political parties, bosses, machines, chambers of commerce, credit

associations, labor unions, factories, newspapers, churches, schools,
welfare agencies, philanthropic societies, humane societies, museums, art galleries, lodges, zoos, auditoriums, parks, playgrounds,
slums, red-light districts, riversides or park avenues, main streets,
jungles, sanitation plants, and taxi-cab companies?"

"One may find anything or everything in the city texts except
the informing principle that creates the City itself. . . . Everything
is present except the one precise essential that gives life to the
whole. When all is said and done the question remains, What is
the City?" (*Ibid.*)

In our ecological development to this point we have considered
man's relationship with his environment, his adjustment to environmental changes and his purposive interrelationships in directing
governing, and controlling his environmental change. The exigencies of man's adaptation to, and impact upon, his environment have
led us to the abstraction of a total environment. Just as economics
as a science or discipline is only a segment of a broader based social
science the economic environment and material welfare of men
constitute only a segment of the total environment in which man
lives. In our frame, then, the city, in all its complexities, depicts
the total environment of man. The city is the mirror to man. A
theory of urban political economy must be interdisciplinary and
pluralistic in encompassing segmented economics, social, political,
technological, religious, and cultural environmental aspects that
motivate and contribute to man's total environment in the City.
Man's environment is a vibrant, changing, and living thing. In
the past, even the relatively recent past of a generation or so ago,
men were able to shrug their shoulders and merely shake their
heads in perfunctory admonition of most of the evils of city life
because they were powerless to prevent them. (Note the individual
citizen reaction to the prohibition era with its evils and gangster-
ism.) But if the city is truly to be a mirror to man, to the democratic
processes and principles by which he lives, and to his genius for
economic and technological organization, man has no one to blame
but himself if his total environment is hazardous to his own life,
limb, and health.

GOALS AND URBAN PROBLEM ANALYSIS

The relevance of goals in functional economic analysis is a
frequent source of theoretical difficulty, particularly when goals
have unquestioned interdisciplinary characteristics and qualities.
In such community-wide goal formation, the attitudes, beliefs,

and value judgments vary widely among the various subculture groups comprising the urban complex. For this reason, the pulling force of the functional economic system may be exaggerated and accomplishment of economic goals within the parameters of enterprising activities may not be attainable independently of related contributing functional systems. Another aspect of urban goals that adds to complexity for economic analysis is the requirement for clearly defining objectives. Such definition may reduce and narrow the scope of the desired result or purpose so as to mitigate and dilute the inter-disciplinary quality of the goal. This specification may make the narrower purpose applicable to economic system analysis or to economic attainment, but obfuscates the total-environmental interrelationships—social, economic, political, and cultural. Clearly, the logical role for goals in urban problem analysis and urban development is unclear, for behavioral and normative theoretical and empirical interrelationships are not adequately distinguished in an interdisciplinary-determined total environment. At the same time the knowledge explosion (an estimated doubling each nine years since 1940) places man in perhaps his most crucial stance of choice in his experience. For the first time in history, nothing seems impossible any longer. Since everything seems ultimately possible to accomplish, everything must be deliberately chosen. Technology creates urban problems; technology can solve urban problems—the difficulties in solution are hardly technical, but rather are system deficiencies inhibiting corrective actions in our modern economy. Man has the knowhow and the means to adjust to those urban environmental conditions he cannot change and to adjust the urban environment purposively to meet his needs as he perceives them. (See Max Ways, "The Road to 1977," *Fortune Magazine*, January, 1967.)

Ecological Bases for Planning

In relation to his total urban environment man must be ready and adept at responding to change, especially in regard to functional interrelationships of activity systems. The system interrelationships in urban places are so interdependent that a change in almost any activity system—economic, social, political, cultural—generates a change in other activities. Robert Brown offers several activity categories as "ecological instruments of change in relation to urban communities." (See R. K. Brown, "The Ecology of Urban Social Change," *The Ideal City*, Georgia State College, Atlanta, Georgia, December, 1964, pp. 40-44,):

(1) aggregation: the dynamics of population takes place as a result of the (a) birth and death rates, and (b) migration pattern shifts.

(2) expansion: encompasses the space dimension, i.e., the relation between population growth and increasing competition for limited land and sky space.

(3) concentration: the density within a given area, as effected by space functions and the economy of time.

(4) centralization: the grand design of an all-encompassing urban activity system.

(5) segregation: embraces segregation of economic activities, of residential neighborhoods, of housing, of land use, of occupation, and of races. When a community urbanizes there occurs a corresponding growth in segregation. The "natural areas" of segregated classes, races, and functions remain in "dynamic flux."

(6) invasion: territorial encroachment; the evolutionary (although sometimes with the seeming rapidity of revolution), the changing nature, structure, and function of natural functional areas within the urban complex.

(7) succession: the end result of completed invasion as seen through controls exercised through zoning, traffic, and related mechanisms.

Synthesizing the above "ecological instruments of change in relation to urban communities," Max Ways suggests two kinds of planning (loc. cit.):

> To sum up: a society committed to radical and unending change has a deep-seated need, previously almost unknown, to develop a sense that it is able to choose its own path by the light of its own values. . . . Nations dominated by ideologies, confident that their problems have been solved by the law of history, can seem to justify this need by a coercive central planning structure that, in fact, drains off the possibility of planning from all parts of society except the group at the top. . . . Several elements of the U. S. problem have been inherent in the way science itself is organized. Tremendous social complexity follows from the specialization of knowledge. Tremendous social frustration and confusion are by-products of science's legitimate effort to become objective. What we have needed is a non-coercive system that will bring the appropriate sciences to bear more effectively upon practical problems and at the same time put more scientists into an organized, intellectually coherent contact with the debate over values and goals. . . .

The new style of dealing with the future offers to millions of living Americans an opportunity far more significant than material progress. Since Socrates, at least, Western civilization has respected the examined conclusion, the conscious conclusion, the conscious connection between thought and action, the intentional life. That we are now developing a set of more effective methods for shaping the future represents a fundamental advance along a main line of social and individual evolution. That most of our public and private planning is and will continue to be directed toward material ends should not mislead anybody into supposing that there are no supramaterial elements involved in the process itself. By 1977, the U. S. should understand more clearly that its highest satisfactions are derived from the way we go about forming our choices and organizing our action, a way that stresses persuasion over force and arbitrary authority, a way that extends to more and more men shares of responsibility for the future. By 1977, it may be clearer that we are not just pushing a material "more"; that what matters to us is how we formulate our goals and how well we pursue them; that in worldly progress, as in another, the distinction is inseparably bound up with the way.

What is the City?

Martindale posed this question. It seems clear in what he himself discusses, in the ecological categories furnished by Brown, and in the insights of Max Ways that the city is something more than physical, something more than organization, something more than spiritual; the city is all these things—a total environment.

In the next 32 years, the urban population will nearly double. Somehow in the U. S. we tend to take for granted that the total urban environment will take care of itself; the facilities, both public and private, and their financing and provisions will appear in time as needed. As part of its inquiry into the basic economic aspects of human resource investment, the Subcommittee on Economic Progress of the Joint Economic Committee of the Congress undertook an examination of the provision of State and local public facilities by public and private agencies and the availability of credit and other resources to finance them. (See *State and Local Public Facility Needs and Financing*, 89th Congress, 2nd Session, Joint Committee Print, December, 1966.)

What the study accomplishes is (1) a quantification of capital requirements insofar as they relate to public facilities, (2) a measure of the apparent gap between these requirements and prospective private credit resources, (3) a provision of basic "universe" data

PUBLIC FACILITY NEEDS

Projected Capital Outlays
of State and Local Public Agencies

(Dollars in Millions)

	1965 Actual	1975 Estimated To Meet Needs	Percent Increase in Annual Outlays 1975 vs 1965	1966-75 Estimated 10-Year Total
BASIC COMMUNITY FACILITIES				
Regional and river basin water supply systems	$2	$30	1,400%	$170
Public water supply systems	1,040	2,250	116	19,440
Rural-agriculture water supply systems	*	140	*	1,100
Sanitary sewer collection systems	385	1,090	183	7,750
Storm sewer systems	417	1,820	336	16,000
Water waste treatment plants	625	1,240	98	9,830
Solid wastes collection and disposal facilities	130	270	108	2,170
Electric power	766	1,350	76	12,250
Gas distribution systems	44	70	59	550
Subtotal, basic community facilities	$3,409	$8,260	142%	$69,260
TRANSPORTATION FACILITIES				
Highways, roads, and streets	7,782	15,330	97	121,650
Toll bridges, tunnels, and turnpikes	388	500	29	4,000
Offstreet parking facilities	102	300	194	2,400
Urban mass transit facilities	242	960	297	7,600
Airport facilities	261	530	103	4,980
Marine port facilities	159	50	(−)69	430
Subtotal, transportation	$8,934	$17,670	98%	$141,060
EDUCATION FACILITIES				
Public elementary and secondary schools	3,650	4,480	23	35,500
Area vocational school facilities	**	790	*	6,300
Academic facilities for higher education	915	1,750	91	13,870
College housing and related service facilities	301	720	139	6,080
Educational television	5	30	500	230
Subtotal, education facilities	$4,871	$7,770	60%	$61,980
HEALTH FACILITIES				
Hospitals		480	*	3,930
Clinics and other outpatient facilities	494	100	*	810
Long-term care facilities		130	*	1,060
Community mental health centers		220	*	1,470
Facilities for the mentally retarded	34	130	282	1,070
Health research facilities	*	240	*	1,920
Medical and other health schools	*	360	*	2,880
Subtotal, health facilities	$528	$1,660	214%	$13,140
RECREATION AND CULTURAL FACILITIES				
State and Federal outdoor recreation facilities	313	530	69	4,400
Urban local outdoor recreation facilities	360	2,200	511	17,600
Arenas, auditoriums, exhibition halls	600	910	52	7,200
Theaters and community art centers	*	460	*	3,620
Museums	14	40	186	270
Public libraries	103	240	133	1,910
Subtotal, recreation and cultural	$1,390	$4,380	215%	$35,000

PUBLIC FACILITY NEEDS (continued)

(Dollars in Millions)

	1965 Actual	1975 Estimated To Meet Needs	Percent Increase in Annual Outlays 1975 vs 1965	1966-75 Estimated 10-Year Total
OTHER PUBLIC BUILDINGS				
Residential group care facilities for children	*	70	*	560
Armories	1	15	1,400	150
Jails and prisons	*	120	*	920
Fire stations	191	170	(−)11	1,370
Public office and court buildings	218	400	84	3,250
Other	214	*	*	*
Subtotal, other public buildings	$410	$775	89%	$6,250

*Not available.
**Included in Public Elementary and Secondary Schools.
Source: "State and Local Public Facility Needs and Financing"; Joint Economic Committee of the Congress; December 1966, Vol. 1, pp. 24-25.

inputs to be used in connection with the planning, programming, budgeting systems being implemented throughout governments and private enterprise, and (4) a provision of new dimensions for the "shelf" of emerging and unmet public facility needs of our urbanizing society.

In his message to the Congress, "Problems and Future of the Central City and its Suburbs," March 2, 1963, President Johnson declared:

The City is not an assembly of shops and buildings. It is not a collection of goods and services. It is a community for the enrichment of the life of man. It is a place for the satisfaction of man's most urgent wants and his highest aspirations. It is an instrument for the advance of civilization.

These words again add substance to the concept of the city as those constituents comprising man's total environment.

The President further declared:

By 1975 we will need over two million new homes a year. We will need schools for 10 million additional children, welfare and health facilities for 5 million more people over the age of 60, transportation facilities for the daily movement of 200 million people. . . . Among the most vital needs of our metropolitan areas is the requirement for basic community facilities—for water and sewerage. Many existing systems are obsolete or need major rehabilitation. And population growth will require a vastly increased effort in the years ahead. . . . A community must offer added dimensions to the possibilities of daily life. It must meet the individuals most pressing needs and provide places for recreation and for meeting with neighbors. (H. Doc. No. 99, 89th Congress, first session, March 2, 1965).

PLANNING, PROGRAMMING, BUDGETING SYSTEMS

An assessment of needs, public or private, can result in considerable refinement and reevaluation of the anticipated and projected needs. Translation of needs into actions and actual undertakings does not become effective unless and until the needs are subjected to comparative economic cost–benefit analyses. Robert W. McNamara initiated the managerial technique of Planning, Programming, Budgeting Systems when he was appointed Secretary of Defense in 1961. PPBS restructured all planning and procurement around missions, objectives, or programs. Through PPBS techniques McNamara achieved effective coordination among the four services, more "bang" for the taxpayer's dollar, and introduced a major advance in administration techniques applicable to managerial functions universally. Application of simple marginal techniques to cost-benefit analyses proved an effective means of exercising and implementing decisions of choice. In 1965 President Johnson directed that PPBS be adopted by all departments of the federal government. The techniques have been found useful in planning and implementing foreign aid assistance projects, in organizing and administering the peace corps, and are increasingly being adopted by local levels of government and by private enterprising firms.

Since the depression of the 1930's and the use of public works as a fiscal device to stimulate employment and create income, economists have postulated the need for a "shelf" of planned public works, the implementation of which would provide a direct means of counteracting recessionary tendencies within the economy. The employment impact of such construction activity is significant, and if the nation meets fully its public and private facility needs in the next three decades, the creation of jobs to meet the needs of a growing labor force will be facilitated. The Bureau of Labor Statistics estimates that each million dollar annual expenditure for construction creates approximately 100 jobs for the year—about 40 jobs at the construction site and about 60 in industries providing the building materials, equipment, and services. To this we must add the multiplier effect, that is, the secondary and tertiary impact of basic income creation and distribution. When wages and salaries are received as facility construction is implemented, retail sales increase, services of all kinds are demanded; indirectly another 50 to 100 full-time jobs are added to the economy. This, it is estimated, means that for each $1 billion spent on urban facility construction, both public and private, some 100,000 jobs are created on the site and in the production and distribution of materials and equipment. Somewhere between 50,000 and 100,000 more jobs augment the labor market as a result of increased sales of goods and services to consumers. With the growth of the labor force in urban centers, these employment needs will grow. PPBS and an estimate of how much capital expenditures for public facilities will have to be increased serve as an essential tool to assist us in anticipating urban environmental needs in the coming decades. Ecological processes accelerate in their urgency as population centers intensify their concentration.

THE PUBLIC MARKET

PPBS as a new style of planning and problem solving assists in the projection of urban environmental needs. However, if the role of government is strengthened in preparing for tomorrow, is this not, as Schumpeter would charge, antagonistic to the private enterprising sector—business? It will not be and should not be, for governments "get things done" through activities of private enterprise. With programmed public facility construction needs, business-government dealings are inviting indeed. This highlights what is euphemistically spoken of as a "private sector" and a "public sector." At the local level of economic activity, particularly, the relationship is one of cooperative, integrative, and direct partnership.

Although the distinction between public goods and private goods in the urban complex is rapidly becoming less distinct and obscured, one typical method of distinguishing has been to divide public and private expenditures for goods and services by dividing them as a relative percentage of expenditures comprising the net national income. In 1965 such a division allocated 20.7 percent to the government sector—federal, state, and local; the remaining 79.3 percent is designated as private expenditure. In 1967 the proportions were government 22.4 percent; private 77.6 percent. Of course the police actions in Viet Nam swelled the public share. In 1965 of the total 136.4 billion spent by governments for goods and services, only 68 billion or about 37 percent went for direct general government performance of services. The rest went for purchases of goods and services from the private enterprising sector. What is key for the future is the requisite trend toward the purchase in the public market of more collective utility. Individual urbanites cannot buy better basic community facilities, urban transportation facilities, education facilities, health facilities, recreational and cultural facilities, or clean air or clean water. Governments acting in the collective interest are going to buy these things. Private enterprise exercising its ingenuity and using the most advanced technology will "do the job" and put the facilities in place for the community. Beyond servicing the economic public facility needs of urban communities, the public market also holds unlimited opportunities for private businesses in traditional public service-type activities. The recommendation is being postulated that the Post Office become a non-profit, autonomous, privately-operated corporation in the image of Comsat. Also there seems no reason why private enterprisers should not control traffic flows, collect garbage, dispose of refuse, clean streets, appraise and assess property for taxes, operate kindergartens and day nurseries, provide computer and centralized bookkeeping services. The list is indeterminant, including urbanredevelopment and low-cost housing.

As the urban environment responds to the public facility base projected to 1975 and as the population grows, becomes better educated, more sophisticated, and more politically aggressive, it is probable that additional public facility demands will accelerate geometrically. An estimate of a trillion and a half public funded dollar investment flows in the next 32 years to meet accelerated public facility needs seems conservative and easily defensible to anyone who has studied urban development and expansion. To this, based on the economic premise that "public funded investment flows must necessarily precede private investment flows," we must add privately funded investment flows which add further to urban environment development. Studies of the economic impact of urban renewal activities indicate a multiplier factor of 4 to 6. Thus we can look forward to private capital investment flows contributing to the urban environment directly related to public flows of some six to nine trillion dollars. This spells "opportunity" in business terms. Given viable democratic processes in our metropolitan complexes, the public needs are going to be met. Given, also, a viable growing urban economy and rising employment and income levels, the private needs of the public are going to be met. The question is whether or not we will meet the growing needs of a growing urban nation intelligently and within the parameters of a market oriented political economy.

A Re-ordering of Market Orientation

Like many of the species, man is a social animal. He differs, however, in his propensity to "barter and truck." Necessarily, a theory of urban political economy must encompass social-political-economic human behavior. However, in condensing behavioral facets of urban environmental ecology into a theory of markets, it must be made clear that what is involved is an analysis and consideration of markets—not of marketing.

Given freedom of choice in economic affairs and assuming that mobility and change are normal attributes of the urban environment, it becomes increasingly difficult to forecast values of economic variables. Equal difficulty is encountered in anticipating social and political values derived from basic economic variables in the urban place. Economic variables are valued and measured through marketplace transactions. Emphasis shifts to the highly monetized characteristics of the urban environment. Every human action that is monetized, although it may serve seemingly a purely social, political, cultural, or religious cause or purpose, is measureable through market transaction mechanisms. Economic monetary flows through the consumer goods market and the producer goods market measure the total of expenditure flows and income producing flows. The behavioral patterns measured reflect the one measure we have available of total human behavior including social, political, cultural, and religious patterns. This is not to say that monetary value measurements exactly reflect or measure social or cultural values; such measurements do, however, provide a relative value judgment as to society's relative desires. Economic measures cannot do more than reflect society's relative judgments. While economic flows do not evaluate social or cultural goals, the economic market measurements do reflect the scope of the means allocated to attain relative goals.

Ecologists tell us that little things count. Every time it rains or doesn't rain, every migration of birds to the south or north, every oil tanker polluting our ocean shores as it discharges its wastes, every auto trip into the city, all add to the ecology of environmental adjustment by organisms living within that environment. In economics, little things count also. Every dollar spent or saved, every dollar hoarded or invested, every dollar taxed and spent for collective consumption or social overhead capital investment, every dollar income generated in one economic activity or another, all through market transactions reflect human behavioral patterns in man's continuing adjustment to the urban environment.

Urban environments are of such pervasive sensitivity to all human behavioral changes that counteracting changes keep the environment in continuing flux. Change is a function of both endogenous and exogenous factors which determine and condition the quality of urban environments. These are, in turn, measured through the market. Changes in the technical feasibility of location of certain kinds of manufacturing or other kinds of processing activities, shifts to recreation-oriented industry, shifts to suburbia from downtown, and the creation and spread of slums are reflected in market processes. Associated with such shift changes might be an entirely different mix of skills in the labor market requirements, a different mix of housing needs, different income and educational attributes of the population, perhaps different health requirements and characteristics, different collective-consumption public service needs, etc. All such shifts in mix are reflected in market functioning.

We have determined for the purpose of effective urban analysis that the city is best conceptualized as an "environment." With further refinement, the total environment is subject to analysis through economic market functioning. The strength of this mode of analysis is that it provides a behavioral model. The overall social-political-cultural behavioral environment can be encompassed as a function of the economic means allocated and used to achieve human ends. This analytical approach has considerable appeal due to its simplicity. Use of a conceptualized simulation model provides an excellent tool for treating interacting force action and reaction. In such a framework, the simulation model allows the use of subjective judgment and allows also solution to determined variable interaction as such interaction would be expected to evolve through market functioning. Functional market forces governing market structure and market functioning in effect depict human behavioral patterns in ecological processes.

·· 9 ··

The Ecological Impact of Technology:
"Physical and System"

TECHNOLOGY "builds-in" innovation, creativity, and change to *man's* environment. In its physical substance and intellectual form technology provides the means for accumulating, storing, and retrieving knowledge. In the seminal sense, the ecological relationship between *man* and *nature* is the relationship of *praxis*, i.e., those pragmatic relationships which cause *man* to make and remake his environment to satisfy his changing needs. Human ecology, then, subsumes an integral connection between physical technology and what can be termed "intellectual or doctrinal or socio-economic system" knowledge technology. On every hand is evidence of physical technology which represents the common human modes of work and life styles. No aspect of human behavior is immune from the impact of physical technology, which embodies the knowledges, the skills, and the material purposes of *man*. Thought, as innovator of change through sheer rational intellectual analysis of abstract relationships, brings us the concept of knowledge "system" technology. *Man* institutionalizes and systematizes ideas and ideologies, concepts and principles. This organizational process also affects the human environment and man's knowledge about himself, his society, and his culture. Again, in the seminal sense, institutionalization and systematization of ideologies and conceptualized relationships make men aware of social processes, of discriminatory prejudices, and of social and economic distortions about which they otherwise might remain unaware. *Man's* intellectual creativity, his technological and knowledge skills, provides a force for change. The economics of physical technology equates with the institutional "system" rules governing play of the economic game.

For example:

> Since traffic has been mentioned, let me offer some notions of how a social analysis can modify a technological problem. Suppose we put a high tax on privately owned automobiles in the United States and a low one on leased or rented automobiles. Suppose for the sake of argument we had mammoth networks of Hertz companies (or whatever you want to call them) which would deliver an automobile to your doorstep in five minutes; the individual would have a standard credit card which merely punched the number of automobile hours that he used per week. Under such circumstances we would have very different patterns of use although the technology would remain the same.
>
> The problem is not automobile ownership, but convenient transportation; and the ownership of a private automobile can easily be confused if society equates the two. There are many technological problems to which people interested in technical coefficients have the solutions in terms of that particular game or framework. But their frameworks may easily be wrong. I feel that we would be well advised to direct ourselves to the area of gearing the sociological imagination to the technological imagination. (Martin Shubik, Working Session One: Baselines for the Future, October 22-24, 1965, in *Daedalus*, Journal of the American Academy of Arts and Sciences, "Toward the Year 2000: Work in Progress," Summer, 1967.)

In the context of Shubik's analysis is an affirmation that the organization and system of economic affairs (knowledge "system" technology) equates with physical technology. In both structures knowledge is vested in *man's* technical intelligence and in the design of the socio-economic game and the rules governing its play.

THE PACE OF TECHNOLOGICAL CHANGE

We shall divide economic history into four developmental phases: (1) pre-industrial revolution, (2) industrial revolution, (3) scientific management, (4) modern knowledge technology. The magnitudes of time differences in the first period as contrasted with the following three periods are startling. Depending upon the authority one consults to estimate the length of time *man* has inhabited the earth, the pre-industrial phase occupies something between 200,000 and 1,000,000 years and extends to about 1750 A.D. The Industrial Revolution starts about the middle of the 18th century and terminates around 1900. Scientific management holds the stage until 1946 when the modern period begins.

PRE-INDUSTRIAL REVOLUTION

The measured rate of growth of knowledge technology seems infinitesimal in *man's* initial evolutionary phase. Knowledge acquisition based on experience and passed by word of mouth from generation to generation was nearly impossible to accummulate, store, or retrieve. The introduction of agriculture in approximately 7,000 B.C. lengthened the human life-span from 20 to 30 years, permitted a more sedentary way of life, and probably augmented the store of knowledge in about the same ratio. "It was the transition from food gathering to food growing that makes the first, and without doubt still the greatest, cultural change in the history of mankind, since it made all subsequent history possible." (S. C. Easton, *A Brief History of the Western World*, 1962, p. 4.)

The invention of writing about 5,000 years before the initial period ended improved the accumulation and the retrieval of knowledge technology. Subsequently the innovation of movable type and the printing process in 1448 by Johann Gutenberg increased exponentially the rate of development in knowledge technology.

The social-economic environment which is identified here as knowledge and "system" technology, and which we equate with physical technology, evolved socially from the family to the tribe to the nation and economically from the individual jack-of-all trades to specialization through the craft artisian, the guild, the market, the factory and to labor, professional, and related organizations in a pluralistic society. The 15th, 16th, and 17th centuries witnessed the rise of the market and the national state in human economic and social groupings. Aided by a spate of new inventions, especially in the arts of navigation and production *man* began seriously and purposively to explore his physical and intellectual worlds. Opening up of new lands and new modes of power and travel introduced new goods, metals, and physical production technology to the Western world. Concomitantly, trade and commerce grew rapidly and intellectual "system" knowledge technology and social economic organization assumed an increasingly important role in human affairs and market oriented behavior.

The new Protestantism replaced the international point of view of the Catholic Church with the idea of national inde-

pendence, lent its support to individualism in economics as well
as in religion, and frankly sanctioned the glorification of the
profit seeking motive in mankind. The age old stigma attach-
ing to money making and personal enrichment disappeared in
favor of an entirely new way of looking at life. Trade and
commerce became socially respectable for perhaps the first
time in all history. (J. M. Ferguson, *Landmarks of Economic
Thought*, 1938, p. 27.)

The new socio-economic game that emerged as the eighteenth
century ushered in the Industrial Revolution was the joint product
of physical and knowledge "system" technology.

THE INDUSTRIAL REVOLUTION

While England and Wales supported a population of about 5
million in 1700, and three fourths lived in the country, work and
life styles were moving into nascent stages of ecological change.

> For thousands of years economic processes had been carried
> out in essentially the same manner. Thread was spun and cloth
> woven by hand; this was true of other manufactured articles. . . .
> During the eighteenth century and the first quarter of the nine-
> teenth, various inventions were made which were destined to
> revolutionize the world changing the everyday life of mankind
> more profoundly than anything of previous age. (Harold
> Faulkner, *American Economic History*, 5th Edition, 1943, p.
> 251.)

The flyshuttle increased the weavers' productivity. The spinning jenny added to the workers' ability to produce thread. The
waterframe and mule further increased productivity in the textile
industry. The power loom combined with the new source of power
provided by the steam engine. Power combined with physical
technology in the form of machines accelerated the Industrial
Revolution. Steam power emancipated industry in its choice of
site allowing concentrations of manufacturing operations of allied
and interdependent firms. Technology made possible also urbanization and survival of an interdependent and specialized urban
population. Steam power, for the first time, allowed man to produce a surplus of goods, i.e., more than the producing population
group desired to consume of the particular goods produced.
Steam power provided the transport facilities, speed, and de-
pendability to service the wider markets required by large production concentrations. The demographic shift was now to the
cities. Work and life styles changed as technology changed the

environment; human ecology spelled out the necessary adjustment processes.

The rate of inventions spurted during this phase of development. In a current listing of the 114 most important inventions of mankind, 52 were introduced in this short period of 150 years compared with 28 listed for the previous 200,000 years. (See *Machines*, Life Science Library, *Time*, Inc., 1964, p. 193-195.) These mechanical achievements in physical technology coupled with a doctrinal knowledge ingenuity in organizing the "mix" of resources into effective production units added to *man's* ability to meet his basic environmental and material needs. In the twenty year period, 1879-1900, output per man hour in manufacturing improved by 41.8% and agriculture boosted productivity by 21.8%. This gain in the rate of productivity improvement toward the end of this developmental phase reflects growth from a base that is far above that which existed in 1750.

SCIENTIFIC MANAGEMENT

At the turn of the century America seemed to have achieved the "best of all possible worlds." Railroads spanned the nation; some 198,964 miles of track comprised the system's interlocking network. Value of product of the manufacturing sector alone exceeded eleven billion dollars and the agriculture product was valued at four and a half billion. Telegraph lines joined all parts of the country and linked America with the capitals of Europe. Some 855,000 telephones were in use in America and more than 18,000 internal combustion engines vibrated noisily across the nation on its farms and in its factories. Throughout the period of industrial revolution little critical attention was given to the way entrepreneurs combined resources and managed productive processes. Men were so centered on the wonders of physical technology that doctrinal "system" knowledge technology was left to experience gained through practice.

Frederick Winslow Taylor, the father of scientific management, changed the pattern. He added intellectual, rational analysis to doctrinal "system" technology. "There is one best way and only one best way to do any task at any given moment in time." This was the philosophy expounded by Taylor in his experimentations, his logic, and his writings on the principles of scientific management. Taylor focused on the unison of man and tool, man and machine, man and the "system" which guided and controlled his activities in the production process. Jobs were divided into specific tasks; men became minute specialists; output boomed as productivity improved. The economic game became increasingly more exciting as the rules adapted employee behavior to the changing system and physical technology.

In 1913 the new Ford plant at Highland Park, Michigan, introduced further innovation to wed physical and doctrinal technology. The assembly line technique brought the work to the man and specialized his tasks. Fords own description illustrates the innovated system technology: "The first men fasten four mudguard brackets to the chassis frame; the motor arrives on the tenth operation. . . . The man who places a part does not fasten it. The man who puts in a bolt does not put on the nut; the man who puts on the nut does not tighten it. . . . On operation thirty-four the budding motor gets its gasoline; it has previously received its lubrication . . . and on operation number forty-five the car drives out onto John R. Street." (*Machines*, p. 83-84.) In another illustration (p. 84): "One man, doing the job from A to Z, had turned out the magneto assembly in 20 minutes. When Ford spread the process over 29 operations, assembly time dropped to 13 minutes 10 seconds. Raising the height of the line eight inches brought it within more convenient reach and cut the time to seven minutes. Adjustments in line speed further reduced it to five minutes." Comparable improvements in efficiency were effected throughout the industrial system as the philosophy of scientific management became accepted and practiced.

Economically, Taylor's rationalization of industrial practice allowed a larger output with less input. This was good. However, with a given propensity to consume and glaring imbalances in the creation and distribution of income, the prime economic flows of consumption and investment expenditures were grossly distorted. The economic discontinuities stemming from deficiencies in doctrinal knowledge technology as applied to the socio-economic system eventually joined in unison to so distort economic flows as to plunge the economy into the deepest and longest depression in history. Physical technology continued to provide a means to accumulate, store, and retrieve knowledge. Inability to use physical technological knowledge and capacity to meet human needs must be found in a lack of doctrinal understanding of "system" technology. The necessary ecological adjustments being signaled by a dynamically changing industrializing and urbanizing environment were recognized and acted upon only partially and incompletely. The need to accumulate, interpret, and understand doctrinal knowledge technology in regard to the socio-economic "system" posed the most serious domestic political problem of the depressed thirties.

MODERN TECHNOLOGY

I place the beginning of modern technology in 1946. This was the year during which *man* broke the sound barrier. The speed of progress, the pace of change during *man's* first 200,000 years was so slow as to be almost imperceptible. In the last twenty-two years the pace of change has become so fast as to be incomprehensible. For the first time in human ecological history an individual experiences birth and meets death in different technological eras. On August 6, 1945, an atomic bomb was dropped on the city of Hiroshima, Japan; three days later another atomic blast hit Nagasaki. Both cities were leveled. On August 10, the Japanese Emperor sued for peace. World War II was over. In devastation and war the atomic era was ushered in. (See John W. Oliver, *History of American Technology*, 1956, p. 25.)

Speaking of cybernetics as modern technology pacing change, Robert Theobald submits: "This emerging pattern will set in motion forces of change within the social order, extending far beyond the present or presently predictable applications of the computer. It will affect man's way of thinking, his means of education, his relationships to his physical and social environment, and it will alter ways of living." (*Main Currents in Modern Thought*, Vol. 22, No. 2, November-December, 1965, p. 42.)

The post-war period of modern technology exhibits many trends:

(1) Transportation capability and speed have made the geographical world smaller. Jet transport effectively removed distance as a barrier to trade and tourism. It seems almost an absurdity to recall that the four-engine propeller driven aircraft was first introduced on civilian airlines in 1948, only a short twenty years ago. Economic market penetration and competition between firms and geographical areas evolved sharply as capacity grew and as distance became a matter of time rather than miles. One result is seen in regional intensification of unique comparative advantages and more trade between regions as specialization deepens. Another is to be seen in the changing functions and "transport mix" of the various modes of transportation. What an incongruity, however, that while we can speed an

astronaut around the earth in ninety minutes it requires two hours to get across town during the rush hours.

(2) An increased mastery over energy prompted Dr. Arthur M. Bueche to say: "We are reaching the point, technologically at least, where we can do most anything we want." (The General Electric *Forum*, Vol. IX, No. 3, July-September, 1966, p. 30.) Never before has man had so many choices in energy sources. Atomic power seems to offer most promise to a power-hungry world. That the world is on the continuing verge of power starvation is supported by Saby's discussion in the GE *Forum* (p. 22). "Electric lighting today consumes about 20 percent of the nation's generated capacity. But if we were still using the dim, less efficient incandescent lamp of only a generation ago, lighting alone would require more electrical power today than the entire 1966 generating capacity of the country. So in lighting, as in other technologies, we are constantly challenged to keep pace with changing and ever increasing needs." Robert E. Hollingsworth projects in the same GE *Forum* (p. 19) that total energy consumption is expected to grow by nearly 50 percent by 1980 and by 140 percent by the year 2,000.

Combining nuclear power with cybernetics, U Thant, Secretary General of the United Nations, expresses the realities of unlimited productive powers of mankind using modern tecnology: "The truth, the central stupendous truth, about developed countries today is that they can have—in anything but the shortest run—the kind and scale of resources they decide to have. It is no longer resources that limit decisions. It is the decision that makes resources. This is the true meaning of abundance: not that goods and services are already available and waiting to be used, but that we possess the potential to call forth everything needed to meet our desires." (*Main Currents*, p. 43.) In this context the future of physical technology rests in man's discovery, use, and control of unbounded energy.

(3) Modern technology grants to man the newly-developed power to direct and control life and physical development of animate and inanimate organisms. In 1965 Dr. Herman L. Finkbeiner developed a simple and inexpensive technique for producing amino acids, the "building blocks" that produce the protein molecules. The synthesis of amino acids is one of thousands of innovations emerging in modern technology. Amino acids open up new horizons for medicine, nutrition, and human health. Scientific farming based upon genetically selected stock, controlled soil and food conditioning, and protective environmental control has thoroughly revolutionized the economic game

in agriculture, tree farming, and exploitation of the natural fertility of nature.

(4) New developments in molecular engineering enable man to alter the characteristics of resources and add new properties (and hence new forms and uses) to old materials. Augmented chemical and metallurgical knowledge improve the properties of tensile strength, weight and thickness requirements, heat and corrosion resistance. Synthetic materials developed require different production processes and work force skills. New uses, new properties, and new economic efficiencies in production and end-use have instituted new and sharp competition between established industries and the newcomers. As illustration, aluminum made a $40 million dent in the can market in just three years. In competitive response, the steel industry's new "thintin plate" cuts aluminum's weight advantage from 3 to 1 to about 2 to 1. Technological research is clearly a central force in economic competition in the business community.

(5) Science has contributed also to man's sensory capabilities. Radio astronomy expands man's vision in space. The electron microscope allows exploration of the minute complexities of cellular and molecular structure by some 140 times over the best optical microscopes. As nature is revealed in greater detail and as knowledge is accumulated, more technological opportunities are exposed, merely awaiting further exploration. With technological advances in vision, transportation and war maneuvers are no longer restrained by conditions of darkness, fog, clouds, or rain. Television disseminates educational knowledge, news, and entertainment. The means of mass informational dissemination are present in newspapers, magazines, radio, and television, and are particularly accelerated by the transistor which frees receiving and transmitting technology from fixed sources of power.

Other technological sensory advances are in hearing, touch, power of discrimination, and memory. The latter has been aided by advances in photographic sensitivity, accuracy in reduction and duplication techniques, instantaneous preservation of vision and sound using video tape, magnetic sound tape, and polaroid photography. These new knowledges add new capacity in recording, appraising, and interpreting data accumulated to advance scientific investigation, to study war strategy, to appraise urban social and physical environmental problems, and to rationalize business decisions and to develop economic projections. On the lighter side, football coaches, baseball managers, professional golfers, and band directors are applying these new technologies in a myriad of diverse ways to improve the way they play the socio-economic game they are engaged in.

From Physical to Doctrinal "System" Technology

Dr. Joel Dean, author of *Managerial Economics*, elucidates the proposition that an urbanized, modern society requires not only an inventor and organized research, but also an innovator, whether public or private, who sees the value of the idea and can marshall the resources to organize, finance, produce, and direct it towards some need the public wants fulfilled. Knowledge of physical technology is not sufficient in itself. We need effective doctrinal "system" technology as well. In today's urban framework, the innovation lag seems due more to cultural and socio-economic system practicalities than to physical technology research or engineering inabilities.

It is one thing to possess the physical technology to reduce urban air and water pollution. It is quite another to generate public determination to foot the bill to do the job publicly or to require individuals and firms to behave in such a way as to mitigate the bad effects of their private gain activities. It is one thing to have the physical technology to provide adequate mobility for people and goods in the city and another to achieve a balanced use of the various transportation modes which would achieve optimal mobility patterns. It is one thing to have the physical technology capable of eliminating urban slums. It is quite another to change the rules of the enterprising game to keep society from perpetuating human poverty and misery. In a socio-economic democracy, the disciplines of profit, loss, competition, and social responsibility are strong market incentives guiding and governing enterprising men. Physical technology is converted through economic production processes into low-cost products for mass markets. Properly conceived doctrinal "system" technology working through modified market orientations, compatible with a changing socio-economic environment, must be designed to do the job while enterprising men in both the public and private sectors function as agents of change in a changing world. (For an interesting and challenging insight to our times, see Max Ways, "The Dynamite in Rising Expectations," *Fortune*, May, 1968.)

. . 10 . .

Economic Issues in Urban Transportation

TRANSPORTATION as an economic utility production function is an increasingly vital factor in national, regional, and urban place development. A well-coordinated transportation system lies at the heart of economic market functioning. The transportation system moves goods and people in and around the national markets, regional markets, and semi-autonomous intra-urban-place markets. The transportation system and the mobility it provides determine land use functions, the location of much economic and social activity, the allocation and use of people's time; and it is an important consideration in the framework of economic choice in individual decision-making.

In fulfillment of its prime responsibility for economic organization, the public sector plays its role in transportation system route development and maintenance:

(a) highways and streets are publicly constructed and maintained; (b) major canals and rivers are made and kept navigable by the Army Corps of Engineers; (c) air routes are determined, designated, assigned, and monitored by federal agencies; and major airports are constructed, maintained, and operated by local agencies of government with federal assistance; (d) ocean-going traffic flows through public port facilities and is protected, assisted, and monitored by the U. S. Coast Guard; (e) public support in the form of land grants to the railroads facilitated acquiring rights-of-way and provided a significant public aid to private investment in railroad development.

On public policy bases, the federal, state, and local governments, through investment expenditure of public funds, have undertaken responsibility for basic economic organization through the provision of traffic routes and terminal interchanges for the various modes of travel in the over-all system.

The transportation system that evolved ecologically in the United States is a unique blend of public and private sector coordination. In railroad development, the government assisted through land grants as noted. Governments facilitated growth of the automobile industry with a system of highways, farm-to-market roads, and city streets, plus, in urban places, parking facilities in many instances. Throughout the system, transportation route and terminal exchange facilities for the most part are publicly provided and/or designated. The vehicles (cars, trains, airplanes, ships, barges, etc.) are privately owned and operated by individuals and firms in private enterprise oriented markets. Empirical observation and evidence indicate clearly that economic activity tends to locate at points where the transportation system best meets the needs for the production, processing, storage, and exchange of goods and services. The nature, scope, and geographical location of economic market places are explicitly associated with technological innovations and developments. Implementation of technological innovations into the transportation system is made possible largely by the public sector. The total private-public transportation system investment probably exceeds $450 billion. If passenger costs in autos, commuter rapid transit, inter-city trains, airplane fares, ocean travel, and freight rates in over-the-highway trucks reflected a full economic costing, there would be considerably less personal mobility and freight traffic demand for, and use of, publicly provided transport routes and privately provided transport equipment. Although we do need to organize, finance, and construct additional transport facilities in our burgeoning economy, it is evident that a substantial part of the congestion problems reflects an underpricing policy. Goods and services that are underpriced always experience excessive effective demand, i.e., the *quantity* consumers want to buy at the lower than equilibrium price exceeds the *quantity* that suppliers are willing to supply at that price.

This empirical facet of economic market behavior serves to point out that in our market oriented political economy, people are conditioned to respond to certain market signals. If any economic good (utility combined with relative scarcity) is underpriced, or seems underpriced, consumers respond by purchasing the good in larger than market equilibrated quantities. Because the private marginal cost of freeway use with one's private auto is far less than the total social marginal cost of providing the route facility, the consumer "thinks he is getting a free ride." He has to pay his taxes whether or not he uses the freeway. A market pricing policy charging a full economic costing of the several modes of *intra-urban* transport mobility would tend to level out relative demands for each mode of travel and tend also to reflect the relative costs of each media. Such a price-cost policy fits the market mold. Publicly provided collective goods that can be "priced" according to relative use or benefit derived should be so priced. Particularly, such changes apply to the use of freeways and the private auto. Mass transit railways, busways, and airways are privately managed and priced with full private average costing in mind and a residual profit as the incentive. Pricing-output policies reflecting total average costing would most certainly result in a more balanced transport system usage among the several travel modes.

The mixed nature of public-private investment and functions performed by each sector complicates, and at the same time simplifies, determination of optimal price-output policy which would tend to balance urban transportation model usage. Inasmuch as the public sector controls prices charged by public transportation utilities (subway, busways, taxis, limousines, etc.) and imposes a heavy tax on motor fuels (to a degree pricing the use of the private auto on publicly provided thoroughfares) it can be maintained that in the main marginal cost of using this or that mode of public or private transport tends toward an equality with the price paid for its use at the competitive standard. Controlled returns to private investors and operators coincide roughly with that return sufficient to keep them in the transportation market in preference to shifting their resources to some other economic activity. From the user's standpoint each mode of transport offers a somewhat different product in terms of speed, convenience, comfort, or status. Thus consumers of transport, insofar as usage has an economic inference, will tend to use this or that mode as expressed by the ratio of value of marginal product received to price of product. Insofar as people behave so as to "maximize" their expected returns from given expenditures, a pricing output policy tending toward total average costing would also tend toward an optimal allocation of transport resources and a balanced system usage among the several modes adaptable to the urban place.

THE NATIONAL NETWORK OF HIGHWAYS—BASES OF
ECONOMIC ORGANIZATION

The interstate highway system was initially scheduled for
completion by 1972. As a public works "shelf item" the system
was conceived by economic planners working in President Roosevelt's New Deal programming during the depressed thirties. The
need for the system development to stimulate and facilitate economic growth, and not economic recession or lethargy, led
President Eisenhower to press for requisite legislation in 1956.
Robert Paul Jordan, perhaps over enthusiastically, refers to the
results in developing the interstate highway system as "the greatest
revolution in ground transportation since the invention of the
wheel." "Our Growing Interstate Highway System," *National
Geographic*, Vol. 133, No. 2, February, 1968.) He says that
even with the latest maps, and acknowledging the interstate auto
travel most Americans do, the individual can no more grasp the
immensity of the entire interstate system of highways than an
ant can perceive the skyline of Chicago.

Dramatically, the interstate and intra-urban freeway system
determines the shape and economy of cities. Urban expressways
may displace the homes of thousands of persons across the nation
in urban centers and may disfigure hundreds of neighborhoods.
Critics frequently score state and city planners for "giving way"
to influential political pressures emerging from articulate affluent
neighborhoods to "cease and desist" the disfiguring done by freeways. It seems to be correct that freeway construction has, in instance after instance, contributed to urban renewal efforts. It is
empirically true that freeways are most frequently routed through
slum neighborhoods that are, in effect, economic vacuums. Although thousands have lost their homes and been forced to re-
locate, the economic slum vacuum is the land use area most in
need of economic pump priming; city face-lifting is critically
necessary. Investment flows gravitate to those points where
traffic flows.

The interstate system illustrates this point. The elaborate system of expressways from coast to coast and border to border is
not a reality reflecting the self-indulgence of an affluent, time-
conscious, and mobile people; on the contrary, the U. S. economy
remains the most productive in the world, and the U. S. remains
the most economically affluent society because the interstate as
one subsystem of a viable total transportation system expedites
economic activity, economic-oriented mobility, and easy access

to markets of all kinds. This is the economic reality of the case. The flow of private investment funds along the interstate system, and around airports, has been so massive that the term "strip" city is common to all. The tentacle urban appendages flowing out of one into another urban place typify urban growth. The direct impact of transportation modes on megalopolis shape and structure is evident. Likewise it is toward access-exit points along the interstate system to which private investment has flowed. What was country just yesterday is urbanizing at interchanges. Our economy strives through market development to "service" a mobile people.

Transportation modes and patterns have facilitated urban and suburban development and in so doing have augmented the problems associated with mobility. The economics of the transportation system as currently conceived, organized, and implemented in the nation, in its sub-regions, and particularly within the urbanizing place structure, is reflecting ecological processes calling for a reappraisal and re-evaluation of economic factors and relationships underpinning the system. Gilmore prefaces this reappraisal:

> Transportation inventions make it possible to do things in new ways and in new places and these new possibilities bring changes in the socio-economic system and in the ecological patterns. These changes may never actually occur. Part of this lag in making changes is a result of the cost of providing and using transportation facilities. Part of the lag is a result of the persistance of past traditions. (See Harlan W. Gilmore, *Transportation and the Growth of Cities*, 1953, pp. 145-6.)

TRANSPORTATION AND URBAN MARKET ANALYSIS

In the sense that the transportation system—in all its several modes—in our urban centers is overcrowded, congested, emitting acrid and even unhealthful polluted air, and is excessively physically demanding, boring, and time consuming, an ecological market functioning maladjustment has developed. The transportation system is failing to meet the mobility requirements of the urban environment of which it is such an integral economic part. The nature and extent of the problem can be analyzed, perhaps to indicate the factors with which solutions may be sought, by careful study of the actions and reactions to stimuli occurring in the economic functioning and structure of the several markets comprising the urban environment.

We have moved now to the point of recognizing the market as an institution created by man and operated by participating economic, cultural, and social institutions, government agencies, and individuals as consumers and sellers. Using this market as the central institution, the independent variable, it is possible to exert positive influence by coordinated actions of the public and private sectors. The system deficiencies can be directed toward advantageous behavioral patterns through appropriate market adjustment and signals to which the system will respond. In each instance, pertinent questions arise: (1) *What* transport mobility markets exist in urban differentiated zonal land use sectors; and (2) *What* are perceived as the transportation needs and modes best designed to service each such zonal market? Economic cost benefit and feasibility analyses provide keys to possible solutions.

BASES FOR DECISION-MAKING

Decision-making by individuals and business firms as to site location and market development within the growing urban complex poses a difficult juggling of alternatives. Transportation facility is most frequently the key to decision.

For the family, the prime consideration is the job-getting, income-earning opportunities for family members in the labor market. The route to work, the travel modes available, the time consumed, the physical and mental strain, the relative cost of commuting, and the kinds of work performed are essential considerations. Balanced against this travel to work consideration is the attractiveness of family living in one neighborhood or another. Relative costs and kinds of housing, governmental provided services, social amenities, access to shops, schools, churches, and recreation facilities contribute to family neighborhood "livability." The balance is reached regarding site location for the family when it is recognized as a good and appropriate location in which "to live and to work." Transportation is critical in determining particular site balance for thousands of pertinent family decisions. The economic impact on family expenditure patterns and the shape of the city is apparent.

Business firms similarly consider not only the more obvious elements of land costs, rents, and the ease of physical distribution of goods and persons to and from the site location, but also its ability to attract an adequate labor force at an advantageous cost. This emphasizes market orientation with the firm acting as a buyer of goods and services as well as a seller of goods and services.

This market-oriented decentralized decision-making by individuals, households, and firms in the urban environment constitutes an important "value" in our enterprising political economy, vitalizes market institutional arrangements, and assures a broad market measure reflecting the urban society's needs and desires. Transportation is a vital consideration in the weighing of advantages and disadvantages of alternative opportunities as regards site location, livability, investment expenditures, technological innovation and adaptation, and very importantly, the development of markets encompassing income-producing activities.

SUB-MARKETS AND TRANSPORTATION

Across the United States, inter-city traffic facilities, travel speeds, and costs incurred are the most economically adequate in the world. The unique transportation "problem" is the short haul intra-urban mobility of people and goods. The massive demand peaks, the uncoordinated model facilities, the absence of the flexibility required for the multiplicity of criss-crossing mobility routes, and variations in transportation requirements by kind and quantity require an economic reconsideration of the allocation and utilization of resources both public and private. Concomitantly, an analysis of purpose or needs as reflected in the various market demands for transportation can aid in the urban system developments necessary to meet urban requirements. The persistence of past traditions poses perhaps the greatest single obstacle. However, necessity is allegedly the mother of innovation. In a massive urban market providing hundreds of millions of one-way short-haul services, there exists immeasurable tractability and market accommodation characteristics which encourage, allow, and implement changing consumer behavior through market direction and change.

A general transportation market analysis may be hinged initially on a theory of urban development patterns. A first premise is that urban places have developed along the pattern of rings or concentric zones. At the nucleus is zone #1 or the Central Business District, the CBD. The adjacent concentric ring (#2) is currently a transition zone which, too typically, is the urban slum vacuum area. Neither all inclusive nor exclusive is zone #3 which, within the central city limits, varies from moderate to expensive residential neighborhoods, and optimizes the balance between travel to work and family livability. Zone #4 is the suburbia of satellite cities each with its own zonal qualities and characteristics and the urbanized counties with their special combination of industrial, commercial, and residential neighborhoods.

A second premise is that an axial urban growth occurs as a wedge or tentacle along major transportation facility routes established or designated by the public sector. Thus growth of residential neighborhoods move outward along radial axes. In between, with access to main transportation routes and facilities, industries are established, shopping centers spring up, and urban sprawl complicates further the urban transportation exigencies in the changing urban environment.

A third premise is the trend toward multi-nucleated urban centers. Transportation systems have so influenced urban growth patterns that economic allocation and use of scarce land resources are dispersed among multi-nuclei rather than converging around and in a single CBD. This is a reflection perhaps of diminishing economic returns to site locations in the CBD as land costs rise and transportation mobility becomes less efficient, more costly, and inadequate to meet growing mobility requirements as land use density increases.

If the above premises reflect urban growth and market patterns, an economic composite is possible. Transportation mobility dictates that urban land allocation and use be dispersed around multi-centered nuclei rather than a single CBD. Economic growth and market development, geographically speaking, occurs in a block-like or neighborhood, or industrial park configuration. These multi-nucleated patterns are distorted in form, structure, and market autonomy by the series of wedges that exude from each urban nucleus along transportation routes.

Economically, the ecology of urban market development and change relates directly to the ecology of transportation systems. The solutions to urban mobility problems rest to some degree in market analysis and development. Urban growth reflects market growth and functioning. In many obvious ways an unfettered public-private enterprise market arrangement produced transportation system externalities that became deleterious to the urban environment. What the market created, the market can change, correct, and improve. The rules of the economic game, if conceived and modified rationally, can make the transport game a much better economic game to play. The mobility exigencies of urban environmental pressures must be met forthrightly.

MARKET CONSIDERATIONS IN TRANSPORTATION SYSTEM CHANGE

Economists can point to urban mobility problems as mal-allocation and dysfunctional utilization of resources. The problems stem partly from rapid, haphazard growth directed by a market functioning dominated by short-term individual profit-motive and a relative shortage of public transport route capacity. A key to market functioning in ameliorating mobility problems in urban places is the need for rules of the game exercising a more positive control over the *demands* for each of the various modes of intra-urban transportation. There exists an urgency in planning, financing, and implementing additional public transport capacity in expanding megalopoli. There also exists an urgency to tie all transport sub-systems into a conceptual and functional autonomous, unified whole—a one system concept. With an adequate supply of total transportation facilities available, the demand for the system's services, in the aggregate and by model sub-systems, can be directed and controlled by application of appropriate economic market output-pricing policies and signals.

A. Origin and Destination

Mobility patterns are discernible through compilation of O and D data and interpretation of these data. The travel-to-work routine can be assessed by labor market analyses and census residential analyses. Types of employment and occupations and types of residential neighborhoods are interrelated and reflect income similarities as well as neighborhood and income differences. The "bedroom" satellite city is an urban metropolitan phenomenon. The transportation needs (demands for mobility) of these commuters are quantifiable. This is possible also for any homogeneous residential neighborhood when the proportionate income and occupational employment mixes are known.

Each household is a consuming unit. O and D data relating to household economic shopping behavior, social travel behavior, etc. reflect also a tie to income levels. Frequency of trips, in-trazonal and inter-zonal, in the urban place reflect basic quantifiable data in relative importance. First is the influence on behavior of the level of household income. The higher the level of income the more shopping trips are made inter-zonal, i.e., downtown to shop in the "name" stores and the fewer intra-zonal trips are made to shop for groceries. Income is a factor, also, in the number, kind, and frequently of social, on-the-town recreation excursions.

A second important factor is age and family composition. Income may be primary in determining the number of vehicles available to the family unit, but the frequency and zonal O and D data are more closely related to the number of persons employed, the age and number of licensed drivers, etc., in the household. A more important consideration than one might assume is the effect of education on the frequency of trips and the modes of travel used. In the metropolis, O and D studies associate higher levels of education with greater frequency of inter-zonal travel in relation to both job and shopping travel within the city. O and D data related to recreation pursuits once again reflect primarily income, education, family age, and composition.

B. Surburbanization of Employment

For economic reasons, convenience, and technological factors manufacturing, processing, warehousing, and retail trade centers tend to move from the CBD to outer zonal locations as the function of the central city changes. Suburban employment has grown rapidly while employment in the CBD has stabilized or grown only slowly in the post-war era. While transportation accessibility has always been a factor in residence and business site selection, the rapid urbanizing patterns of the last two decades have disturbed the stability of land use patterns. The urban community has been transformed by pervasive changes in economic efficiencies stemming from innovations in transportation technology on the one hand and route inadequacies and modal inflexibilities on the other. A central and critical economic question facing urban centers is: "Can the market be modified in such a way as to provide a comprehensive transportation system adequate to meet efficiently the economic, social, and political needs of the urban environment?" The massive suburbanization of large concentrations of semi-skilled and white collar service-oriented employees, in income level groupings more compatible with middle income neighborhood intra-city zonal residential lifestyles, accentuates the metropolitan-wide transport problem in servicing a diverse market. At the same time, residential housing developments for medium income groups in the suburban fringe extend metro boundaries along newly-defined lines, intensify housing rehabilitation problems intra-central-city, and emphasize the need to maintain flexibility in transportation system design and development.

Economic Consideration in Market Control

Market functioning from the urban planners' viewpoint must be based upon sound economic principles. Choice must be allowed as the prime force governing the way in which market mechanisms determine price-output decisions. The market serves also to integrate and coordinate the public-private characteristics of the urban transportation system.

The Public Sector in Urban Transportation

In the market place the price mechanism embodies two primary economic forces: supply of the goods or services and demand for goods or services. Price mechanisms also reflect elasticities of price-quantity relationships, price of substitute and complementary goods relationships, income-quantity relationships, and the like. For this analysis both broad forces are involved, although most typically the public sector plays the role primarily of urban transport route and facility supplier. In its role as provider of routes and facilities the public sector organizes the urban environment for mobility inherent in economic activities.

In reference to economic organization the question is posed: "What is or should be the prime purpose and function of publicly provided facilities in each zonal area development of the urban place?"

It is the position of this analyst that different modes of transportation have different economic utilities attached to them in the several different zonal differentiations. A street in each of the several nucleated centers is, and so should be considered as, access to a market place. In the CBD with its massive concentration of governmental, financial, legal, professional, service businesses, the street is a maze of specialty shops, restaurants, and related service enterprises located there to service the CBD human organization working in the multi-storied people boxes.

The peak transportation load on publicly provided facilities occurs as this CBD human business organization commutes into the central zone from suburbia and when the human organization structure collapses at 5:00 p.m. and the massive trek to suburbia begins. One way streets, no parking, controlled traffic movements enforced by police scramble and unscramble this twice-daily massive motorized access and egress from the city centers. The commuter must be serviced but the insistence to serve him in his selected mode of transportation—the private auto—underpins the transport problem and contributes to the malaise of

the street as the legitimate access to market function it was designed to be. The surburban commuter who works in the CBD
contributes much to the cost of city facility provision and administration, and contributes little to its financial support or to
its leadership. Nonetheless, in city planner circles the problem
of serving the commuter in his private auto is paramount. The
merchants who service the needs of the downtown businesses and
employees are encountering difficult economic problems as the
access to their market place is disrupted by an almost psychotic
drive to move the growing multitude of private cars in and out
from suburbia.

One effective means of protecting the market function of
streets in the CBD would be to apply the "plaza" concept to
central intensive land use areas. Less intensively used urban land
space on the CBD fringe could be adapted to parking facilities
and coordinated with access and egress freeways. Mobility within
the CBD would be controlled; goods would be moved only
at off-the-peak load hours. People movement could be provided
by small train-like electric vehicles, for example. Also, to facilitate acceptance, this travel mode might be "free," supported by
local business enterprise. These enterprises already provide vertical
elevator transportation free. In their own self-interest to keep the
CBD economically functional, to enhance its market function,
and to add to downtown attractiveness, the provision of horizontal
transportation free within the CBD boundaries seems a logical
next step.

The multi-nucleated feature of the expanding urban place,
the wedge-like protrusions of the urban growth pattern with the
heterogeneous sprawl between the tentacles and the specific point
concentrations of employment and shopping centers in suburbia
pose serious questions as to the economic feasibility of rapid, underground rail transport. Initial underground rapid transit facilities are extremely costly. Underground rail transit is fast between established geographical points but is both rigid and inflexible in its economic mobility route performance and cost.
To recover its huge fixed costs, massive numbers of patrons are
essential.

The overwhelming proportion of fixed costs to total costs
of rail rapid transit systems is the crux of economic feasibility
analyses. Given massive numbers of commuters, decreasing costs
per unit of transportation are attainable. However, any usage less
than massive means necessarily a less than capacity utilization of

fixed investment facilities; as a consequence per unit costs of transportation rise rapidly. A system with a built in route flexibility, a capacity to handle massive and short-lived peak demands for its services, confronts an almost insoluble pricing-output policy question. With its large proportion of fixed costs, the system must operate. Closing down or cutting back on variable costs through limited service does not materially reduce total costs. Further, as important as transportation is to the commuter, and as costly as it is in time and money, it is difficult to know how a revised pricing schedule that realistically charges the commuter ALL THE TRAFFIC WILL BEAR AT THE PEAK TIME PERIOD and reduces prices sharply during off-the-peak periods would encourage businesses whose employees use the facilities to stagger hours. On the other hand, the problem remains unsolved economically, even assuming the suggested pricing policy is politically palatable. In competition with alternative modes of transportation existing rail rapid transit systems have been losing patrons wholesale for the past two decades. Actions a firm may take while facing a rising demand schedule in a growing market are not those available to the rapid rail transit authorities. Rather, the market problem in the urban transportation system's functioning is how to (1) make rapid transit more attractive, accommodating, and convenient and (2) to shift demands for transit mobility from other competing modes of urban transit to rapid rail transit.

The dispersion of the central city into multi-business centers, a growing trend toward high rise apartment living styles, and integrated autonomous plaza-type developments for work and living, the stabilization of employment in central core cities, and the growing and dispersed employment in specific suburban locations, pose serious doubts regarding the economic feasibility of rapid rail transit underground facilities. Relatively less dense population trends in Central Business Districts and an increasingly dispersed suburbia require flexibility in the system as a prime requisite. Higher income professional, managerial, and white collar persons exhibit strong personal preference for private auto mobility and tend to shun the subway in increasingly larger numbers. Also, employees who form car pools observe a marked decreasing cost per unit of transportation which is not readily apparent—per customer—on the rapid transit. This observation tied to convenience and time savings encourages use of the private auto. And, probably most important, as the urban place develops between main travel corridors, *the rapid rail transit, in its route inflexibility, simply does not go where the commuter wants to go.*

Rapid bus transit requires minimal private initial investment, can service as many high volume mobility corridors as demands for service will support, is flexible in routing and frequency, and can provide a wide range of services to the broad criss-cross urban sprawl areas. Speed in expressway bus travel is attainable with minimal engineering and traffic control planning. Express busways, as an integral part of freeways and city thoroughfares joining the several central business "plaza" centers, and through widening the door to suburbia with all its inter-mobility-corridor sprawl, can offer a marked improvement in the quality of intra-urban mobility. The criss-crossing of traffic between main travel corridors (expressways, main streets, highways, and rapid rail transit lines) and adaptation to changing urbanizing-industrial-izing patterns are easily serviced by flexible busways systems. The proportional distribution of fixed and viable costs again are key to economic feasibility analysis. For the busways, variable costs are proportionately greater. This provides managerial lee-way in adjusting service capacity to fit the peaks and valleys of mobility demands. In this case, the social investment constitutes a large proportion of the fixed costs associated with route and terminal facilities. However, it is recognized that facilities so provided by the public have for the most part a dual use capability. Costs are, as a result, reduced proportionately.

The automobile performs both a status and a transportation function. It is comfortable, time saving, convenient, and relatively competitive in cost. In zones outside the several CBD's, the auto facilitates the economic market function. It carries shoppers and workers from residence to store and job with facility. It is only at points of massive concentrations where serious traffic problems evolve. Surburban industry provides huge free parking lots for employees, and suburban shopping centers provide huge free parking lots for shoppers. In the city, the economics of space limitations and conservation must be recognized and used as the basis for pricing and controlling the types of transportation used and the demands for each. Economic analysis in this case is relatively simple. Study the empirical data, provide the transporta-tion means and facilities to adequately meet the determined needs, and price each mode so as to fully utilize the services of each. Cars can be kept out of the CBD by zoning it as a plaza, or by pricing them off the streets through charging the maximum price the market will bear at the CBD parking garage, requiring special high-priced license permits, higher tax rates, etc. Given adequate parking on the fringe of the CBD and adequate mobility means within the CBD, the auto coordinated with express busways can provide the mobility required in the metropolis. The problem is not wholly one of technology or engineering design or cost. The real problem is "system" and recognition of the economic functions performed by each zonal division in the urban place. Design and control of the best system to service the needs of the markets in the urban environment is essentially a simple matter of economic feasibility among transport alternatives. The comparative costs and advantages of each modal sub-system are measurable and comparable in regard to urban environmental mobility requirements.

An Integrated Total Urban Transportation System

The intra-urban transportation system, if considered within the framework of a functioning market, becomes a simple case of business analysis. Every market is serviced by a going economic organism, public or private. In turn, every economic organism services a market. The urban center conceptualized as a market provides the necessary signals to elicit pertinent economic actions to meet mobility needs. The public-private mixture of interdependencies and responsibilities need not obfuscate the realities of the problem, if only the problem and not the persistence of the "way we have always done things" prevails.

For example, for the metropolitan center, the airport is to be acknowledged as A MAIN STREET—AN IMPORTANT ARTERY OF COMMERCE FOR GOODS AND PEOPLE. Yet, rare indeed, is the urban transit system that integrates air mobility as an integral sub-system in the over-all urban mobility pattern. The way we have always done the job of integrating air travel mobility to and from the airport is traditional. First, the public sector constructs and operates the major airports and provides the access routes (street, highways, and expressways) to the air terminal. On the social overhead base, private enterprisers operate taxis (seats 4) and limousines (seats 8) and limousine buses (seats 50). Customers complain articulately and vehemently in every major airport that it takes more time to find a taxi and get downtown than it does to fly from Chicago. Close to reality now, and posing ground travel congestion problems that tax the intellect of the most creative airport and city traffic manager, is the civilian version of the Lockheed C-5A that will carry 800 passengers. Strain as it might, the old traditional system will no longer suffice. Major urban airports must be integrated into an integrated intra-urban transportation system.

Market signals are sensitive to changing demand and supply relationships in regard to transportation mobility services just as signals tell businessmen to increase or decrease stocks of goods on their shelves or to modify and update their production, promotion, or marketing techniques. Further, market signals differentiate, insulate, and separate markets. We observe these phenomena in "brand name" products, branch stores in suburbia of downtown "name" stores, and "bargain basements" in these same "name" stores recognizing income groupings among customers. Similar signals are evident and quantifiable in the urban transportation market. Mobility demands by transportation mode may be determined for intra-zonal areas and across zonal lines, criss-crossing suburbia and into the core city.

Based, then, on urban growth patterns and quantifiable mobility needs and preferences, the mixed public-private transportation system can be integrated to meet urban environmental needs. Public provision and/or designation of route and facilities through judicious flows of basic social capital investment funds prefaces economic organization in the community and guides mobility patterns. On this basic social overhead structure the "mix" of public and private enterprising transport modes will move people and goods. If allowed to function rationally, market signals will determine price-output relations for each transportation mode. Comparative costs of each can be reflected in demand-supply relationships and prices charged for the various services provided. The guided functioning of sub-modal markets melds the several modes into an over-all market functioning which achieves an integrated transportation system in the urban place. The interaction of public-private interests, responsibilities, and roles played by each in the transportation system can be effectively coordinated through the development and implementation of an autonomous market function for intra-urban transportation.

.. 11 ..

Economic Issues in Urban Housing

In his provocative book *The Future as History*, Robert L. Heilbroner begins his treatise with the following insights:

> History, as it comes into our daily lives, is charged with surprise and shock. When we think back over the past few years, what strikes us is the suddenness of its blows, the unannounced descent of its thunderbolts. Wars, revolutions, uprisings have burst upon us with terrible rapidity. Advances in science and technology have rewritten the very terms and conditions of the human contract with no more warning than the morning's headlines. Encompassing social and economic changes have not only unalterably rearranged our lives, but seem to have done so behind our backs, while we were not looking.
>
> "These recurring surprises and shocks of contemporary history throw a pall of chronic apprehensiveness over our times. (Robert L. Heilbroner, *The Future as History*, 1960.)

The rapidity of change in the work and life styles of an exploding population in an industrializing-urbanizing environment has tended to generate serious "system" maladjustments. Institutional economic arrangements which served a simpler and less charged environment are ill suited to meet the needs of the complex, highly interdependent and specialized work and life styles of the modern urban political-economy. The present unsatisfactory state of urban political-economy, problem-oriented development stems partly from the democratization of political power combined with technological advance and demographic mobility. Joint community-wide investment, production, and consumption functions actuated by urbanites through the democratic processes governing public sector policies are belatedly engaging the historic economic realities of environmental sub-system maladjustments. The public sector, through fulfillment of its primary functions organizes the urban environment for economic, social, cultural, and related

127

human activities. Provision of the basic social overhead capital base to facilitate private economic activity is a public function designed to mitigate environmental maladjustments in the urban place. In the urban problems themselves, and in the usual conceptualized solutions, traditional economic, political, and social systems are reflecting turnabouts and shifts in expectations in the orderly processes of economic, political, and social affairs. In our analyses here, sub-system analysis offers a facility and means with which men can grapple freely with the economic issues that beset the over-all urban environment. The issue here is to define and recognize urban housing problems for what they are pragmatically.

In a survey of business executives regarding the urban business environment, Sternlieb reports an attitudinal pragmaticism: "A clear majority have no great faith in the growth of downtown real estate values while a sizeable minority feel that long-term investments in the downtown area make little sense. . . . The necessity for effective marketing programs to rejuvenate the image of the city, as well as urban renewal efforts to modernize its physical aspects, coupled with enlightened leadership to improve municipal administration is very clearly evident in our survey." (George Sternlieb, "Is Business Abandoning the Big City?", *Harvard Business Review*, January, 1961, pp. 160, 164.)

In the same survey an executive is quoted as saying, "School buildings and highways are very important, but equally significant is pride in being a citizen of a great city. If we can build that feeling in a city's inhabitants, they will rebuild continually. It is in this area that business executives are most needed to give leadership." (*Ibid*, p. 164.)

Perhaps "enlightenment" of progressive business leaders will serve to solve the growing malaise of sub-system market maladjustments with regard to environmental needs. A closer, more intimate, and better coordinated political-economy game combining more integrated action of the public and private sectors seems inevitable.

A Case of Entrepreneurial Enlightenment

Urban housing, particularly low cost housing, is an economic issue of significant import. "Enlightenment" such as was reported by Eugene Patterson (Editorial, *Atlanta Constitution*, January 23, 1968) reflects a businessman's judgment and motivation which may contribute to a market-oriented solution to low cost housing problems.

I've been visiting the homes of some of my employees. Some of the conditions made me sick. Ninety dollars a month and no hot water—and the girl who lives there is white, incidentally. My dog lives in a better house than some of the Negroes.

The government can't do it. Not all of it, and not in time.

I think there are a lot of other businessmen who feel the way I do, if you'd given them a chance to show it. Give them the hardheaded leadership and the organization to make some impact and I think you'd find they're ready to move. They're worried too. Not so much about riots as about knowing they're sitting back doing nothing when they know things need to be done—things that affect their consciences and their pocketbooks too.

There are plenty of others—too many—who don't know or don't care. But I know. You don't have to be a genius to know that a man living in a dungeon doesn't look at things the way you and I do. When you get something, you want to keep it. When you've got nothing, you don't care. Law and order means a different thing to you and them.

I believe men were put in this world to work. But if you don't do anything about opening up a chance at a better house or a better job to them, you ought not to be surprised when they come boiling out of that dungeon. Try and hold the lid on people who've got nothing to lose and you're making a revolution.

I want to do something. My Christianity and my self-interest are both going to get hurt. Why can't somebody get together all the businessmen who feel the way I do and say, "Look, we're going to get some houses built and some jobs opened up for these poor people, and we're going to see that it's done ourselves."

Perspectives on Enlightenment in the Public Sector

Increasing concern about housing the nation is evident also in the public sector. In 1937 President Roosevelt observed that one third of the nation's people were ill-housed. Poor families could not with their earning power buy adequate housing in the private market. Roosevelt pressed for and Congress passed that historic legislation which launched the Public Housing Program. Legislation providing for public low-rent housing to fill a growing breach in the private housing market initiated significant new rules of the economic game. Basic human survival needs can no longer be left to chance (and apparently to an unfettered private market functioning) in the modern, urbanized political economy.

In 1949 President Harry Truman and the 81st Congress provided for urban renewal efforts and pledged "as soon as feasible

. . . a decent home and a suitable living environment for every American family."

During President Kennedy's THOUSAND DAYS legislative efforts broadened the role of the federal government in "somehow augmenting" the supply of lot cost housing to low income families. In 1962, by executive order, President Kennedy banned racial discrimination in all federally aided housing.

President Johnson, during his administration:

(1) Established the Department of Housing and Urban Development bringing scattered housing and urban development programs together for coordinated administration.

(2) Established a program of Rent Supplements to aid needy families in exercising a demand for moderate priced housing in the private housing market.

(3) Inaugurated the Model Cities program, designed to be eventually a massive attack on urban blight including basic survival needs—health and housing.

(4) Established broad national goals in the Housing and Urban Development Act of 1968. In his message to the Congress, the President set goals to meet a massive urban housing need: the construction of 26 million new homes and apartment units over the next ten years, the rehabilitation of 2.35 million housing and related blight reduction and neighborhood improvement recommendations.

Public Law 90-284, 90th Congress, HR 2516 enacted April 11, 1968, provides that it shall be unlawful "to refuse to sell or rent after the making of a bona fide offer, or to refuse to negotiate for the sale or rent of, or otherwise make unavailable or deny, a dwelling to any person because of race, color, religion, or national origin." Open housing became with this Act a legal reality, if not yet an economic or social reality. However, the rules of the housing market game are in the flux of change.

The Department of Housing and Urban Development (HUD) provided a needed administrative centralization of federal efforts to revitalize the urban core of the American economy. HUD acts in four prime areas: (1) urban renewal; (2) rehabilitation; (3) public low-rent housing; (4) model cities programming. Through a broad-based system of grants HUD works through local government officials, private builders and realtors, non-profit sponsors of multi-unit housing, and rent supplements. HUD provides funds also for improvements in neighborhood facilities, urban beautification, open spaces and recreation, college multi-unit housing, and broad aspects of community planning.

Notwithstanding the attitudinal enlightenment of progressive business leaders and, in relation to critical environmental requirements, niggardly funding and something less than adequate direct action by all levels of government, the task of retarding urban blight is not yet truly begun. The real problem of attaining viable revitalization and refurbishment of our major urban centers remains critical. In those economic forces determining the real estate market structure and investment expenditure flows appear the most promising solutions. Regarding progress to date, Montgomery states: "The elaborate array of special-purpose institutions created to supply low cost housing and urban renewal services on behalf of slum dwellers simply has not worked." (Roger Montgomery, "Notes on Instant Urban Renewal," *Transaction*, Vol. 4, No. 9, September, 1967.)

Market Performance in the Post-War Decades

Americans have found that "it takes a lot of dollars to make a home." During the decade 1948-1957 some $227 billions of dollars flowed into the long-term money market. Of this total, residential mortgages absorbed some $88 billions compared with $70 billions for non-residential mortgages, and $34 billions for state and local government securities. These relationships seem important as a means of emphasizing the strategic investment role residential housing plays in maintaining a dynamic and urbanizing economy.

Market instability which characterizes the market for new residential construction may provide an insight to means to adapt the housing markets' functioning so as to stimulate the right signals and in this way to encourage an enlarged production of low cost housing. During the period 1948-1957 the number of private housing starts under VA and FHA auspices varied in a single year as much as 46 percent on the up side and 40 percent on the downside. Under VA, taken alone, housing starts have risen 95 percent and fallen 53 percent in one year. Housing starts increased 37 percent from 1949 to 1950, dropped 25 percent from 1950 to 1951, rose by 13 percent from 1953 to 1954, rose another 9 percent from 1954 to 1955, and fell 17 percent from 1955 to 1956. Instability continued into the 1960's. From 1960-1964 non-farm housing starts rose 12 percent and from 1964-1966 dropped 24 percent. The fluctuations in market behavior are most apparent in the government guaranteed mortgage market where supported interest rates tend to be quite inflexible.

Market instability which marks new housing starts seems incongruous in an urbanizing economy and one in which long-term credit is remarkably steady in year to year movements. However, the flows of credit into the several segments of the long-term capital market fluctuate widely. A striking inverse relationship has existed in the last two decades between capital funds investment flows into industrial securities and residential mortgages. Industrial users desiring to borrow capital funds in the long-term capital market are in a stronger position to bid for funds because it is they who can best exercise the initiative; they, who are the most flexible; and they, who are the creators and productivity improvement implementers. Being more flexible and better able to put investment capital to earn and to pay for itself, enterprise can outbid individual residential mortgage borrowers. The latter are residual claimants when business demands for long-term investment funds lag.

MARKET ORGANIZATION STRUCTURE

Construction, particularly residential housing production, is a decentralized, economically disorganized industry. The market structure is characterized by a relatively few big builder speculators (Levittown) and large numbers of small local (three to ten houses annually) entrepreneurs. Feast and famine levels of residential construction have both their economy-wide costs and rewards. Used as a counter-cyclical device, housing has provided a mechanism for both braking and accelerating the levels of overall economic activity. At the same time such erratic market performance has contributed to much in and out movement of marginal contractor-builders and development of what one official in the industry refers to as the contractor mind. In a private response to an inquiry regarding the feasibility of attaining larger quantities of low cost urban housing an official stated:

> I think the biggest problem in getting low cost urban housing is to get the contractor mind out of the problem. I do not believe that the solution lies in any sudden technological breakthrough, building systems or what have you. The problem is that as long as the contractor mind is in control, emphasis will be on "what is there in it for me?" rather than "what can be cut here without sacrificing basic quality?" Contractors, architects, and others in profit making businesses tend to be reimbursed on something like a percentage basis. When the cost begins to approach a point

where the time and effort are too much for the return, there is no incentive to press the matter further . . . not that there is any deliberate decision, just a general lack of incentive . . . the construction people are right out of the profit making mold and tend to follow the old ruts with shameless persistence.

Economic organization of the construction market, particularly that of residential housing, is occurring notwithstanding its local nature and characteristics. Levitt and Sons, the intrepid builder of mass housing, was acquired by International Telephone and Telegraph in 1967. Technological developments in pre-cutting and pre-fabrication by a growing number of large firms such as the Jim Walters Corporation and National Homes further substantiate oligopoly characteristics in the market structure. In the organizational trends of the housing industry toward bigness may lie those solutions necessary to stimulate market provision of greater quantities of low cost housing. Certainly, planned "new cities" to be built by the General Electric Company, General Dynamics, and other well-known conglomerate firms give a new look to market structure and organization in the construction industry.

On the demand side, housing has a tremendous growth potential looking forward to the 1970's. An average of 2,000,000 housing starts a year is perhaps minimal. For an industry presently geared with capacity for 1,500,000 new housing units annually, the outlook is for growth—by 33 percent productive capacity at the minimum. The war stimulated population explosion is moving into the age grouping most active in the new housing and apartment market. Marriage and family formation is a potent stimulant to residential housing construction. The 1970's will witness net household formation of 1.25 million per year. In 1955 the typical suburban house was 500 square feet smaller than it was in 1968. The trend toward upgrading in size, convenience, comfort, and quality is reflected in rising family incomes of suburbanites and in rising costs of residential construction.

Significant in relation to organization, structure, and performance of the building industry is the fact that from the 1930's to 1968 the industry experienced not only urban real estate development, but also an unprecedented monetary development. That a business friend purchased a home property in 1937 for $10,000 which he sold in 1968 for $40,000 seems in no manner to reflect anything that occurred in the real estate itself. The house is 30 years older, the neighborhood is not any better except it is now closer to downtown than it used to be. The reason the price on the property moved upward can be expressed succinctly—INFLATION of land prices accompanying urban growth and rising construction costs. In urban centers across the nation an authoritative estimate is that somewhere near 75 percent of all urban developed land is now accommodating its original urban structure, i.e., the present land use represents its first departure from the use of that same parcel of land for agricultural purposes. Raw land at the urban fringe available at low cost provided ample quantities of grist for the mill of small, medium-sized, and large land-developer-speculative builders.

THE HOUSING MARKET IN FLUX

During the last six years, says economist Michael Sumichrast of the National Association of Home Builders, "land values have increased by 15% annually. Too, in 1967 the cost for building the shell of a house was $13.90 per square foot compared with $13.20 in 1963. (As quoted in "Housing: The Boom that Must Come," *Dun's Review*, March, 1968.)

Two revealing statements in the same article are indicative of diverse trends affecting the residential housing market:

> By continually outdating the house of the present, the home builders literally build obsolescence into the home and whet the consumers' appetite for a new one . . . a truth that nobody seems to understand is that yesterday's house is as obsolete as yesterday's car. (*Ibid*, p. 34.)
> Levitt's Wasserman, for one, sees housing prices rising 7% a year over the foreseeable future, principally because of climbing land and labor costs . . . and for the consumer with that little dream house in mind there is one more good reason to consider buying now: his own income which has risen less rapidly than home prices for some time, may fall further behind. (*Ibid*, p. 36.)

Out of the economic flux reflecting consumer tastes, consumption, and home investment patterns is the trend toward the mobile home. Americans are a mobile people and as life styles change so also have tastes in living accommodations. Nationally, mobile homes provide about one-third of all housing priced under $10,000. (See A. A. Ring, and N. L. North. *Real Estate Principles and Practices*, sixth edition, 1967, especially Chapter 27, "Real Estate and the Mobile Home.") Significantly accelerating the mobile home trend, I think, is the capacity to incorporate modern home technology in compact, inexpensive mass produced housing units. Also, the mobile housing explosion (every sixth new house in the U. S. was reportedly a mobile home in 1968) reflects an economic push given a sector of private industry by the inter-state highway system. About 100,000 jobs have been created in mobile home production and sales. Charles Dole, in the *Christian Science Monitor* ("The Pumpkin turned into a Coach," April 15, 1966, p. 11) reports on the mobile home trend. Sales doubled from 1960 to 1965 and the 70 foot by 12 foot popular model becomes easily mobile on four-lane expressways. Retail sales reached $1 billion in 1965. However, Ring and North indicate that because of the size of the home and the cost of trucking the motto of the mobile home industry seems to be "less mobility and more home for your money." (*Ibid*, p. 439.) In this instance, economies of scale in mass production and the incorporation of modern home technology in compact, comfortable, and relatively inexpensive housing units offers an attractive product for a large segment of the housing market. Also, Ring and North indicate that mobile home dwellers tend to have higher income per family and more formal education than the national average.

Economically, the mobile home joins the "second car" as an adjunct of rising family incomes and changing life styles. The mobile home as the "second home" at the lake, the beach, or in the mountains is a familiar sight. As a renewable housing tech-nology and as a movable housing facility, mobile housing may provide a most satisfactory and economical means of adding flexibility to environmental urban housing requirements while, at the same time, facilitating adaptation to changing land use functions as the urban environment develops and redevelops. Urban planners have another tool and facility at their disposal.

LAND RE-USE: WAY OF THE FUTURE

Urban sprawl, the spread to a heterogeneous suburbia, encom-passing a broad spectrum of "cracker-box living" styles in an uninspiring standardized conformity represents the land develop-ment of the post-war era, made possible by the mobility provided principally by the automobile. Percentagewise, suburbia continues to grow; land development accommodating the original urban structure continues, but abatement in sprawling growth rates seems just around the corner. The frontiers in the urban real estate industry lie in land re-use, not in original urban use and continued urban sprawl. The inevitable land re-use development will provide a means to adapt to changing urban requirements. The process is going to be difficult and traumatic for it will tend to bring about a restructuring of the industry. It will tend to shake out the small marginal developer-builder. It will require improved management organization and administration, improved financing techniques, and uninhibited creativity and innovation. Entirely new concepts, industrial organization, technology, and changed market structure are essential to assure that the private enterprising system can profitably transform a problem of social and physical malaise into an economic opportunity. Environmental market signals are prompting an organizational and technological response toward bigness. The rules of the game change as the game changes to meet environmental exigencies. Provision of low cost housing by the private market is an unremitting pressure; otherwise public low-cost housing may well replace the private market entirely in this portion of the housing market to the detriment of the total private enterprising system. Private low cost housing is one pressing human need the private market must meet if the free enterprising system is to resist further government encroachment.

There are, I would estimate, some thirty million houses in this country that have not been painted in ten years. Translated into gallons of paint, this means a good market for 750 million gallons of paint. Probably nine million houses in which people live have no hot water. This, at the very minimal American standard of life, is a basic necessity. Probably three million houses lack even cold water piped inside. And there will be some 14,000 cases of medical treatment for rat bites and infections in American urban slums this year.

These incongruities in an affluent urban society are morally and socially intolerable. The daily press confronts every thinking citizen with the deleterious social and political repercussions stemming from these urban residential economic wastelands. The answer to this social and physical malaise lies not in welfare but rather in education and hard-headed economic neighborhood development within a dynamic market functioning calling the right signals.

BARRIERS TO THE PRODUCTION OF LOW-COST HOUSING

We have suggested that the organizational structure and technological investment requirements of the building industry are changing. The change is toward bigness and corporate enterprising actions to overcome market barriers inhibiting large-scale, low-cost housing production.

Prominent barriers are:

(1) *Ineffective, ill-inforced, outmoded, and inhibiting urban building codes*

One prime incentive for the conglomerate firm to "build a new city" is the absence of inhibiting, inefficient building code restrictions. Large firms, planning large renovation projects in urban places, are able to secure political accommodation to modernization of codes more readily than can the small developer.

(2) *Union work rules*

Production bogies, output limits, inhibiting specialized craft rules are allegedly pervasive in building trade unions. That this should exist as a means of insulating jobs, employment levels, and income from the vicissitudes of market competition is not unexpected. The problem now is, can the rules be relaxed or changed to meet the critical housing problem facing urban America? Indications are that large firms negotiate effectively with union leaders who are increasingly cognizant of the urgency of the problems facing them, the industry, and the nation.

(3) *Rising land values*

Transportation system inefficiencies are tending to retard continued outward fringe housing developments except for housing which supports suburban factories and suburban employment and that accompanying strip city developments. Low cost housing in shortest supply is in the land re-use areas of the core city. In this instance, the changing nature of the function of the CBD, the core city itself, and the propinquity of specific geographic areas to urban functional processes are acutely important in land re-use planning. In slum areas, the residential housing and apartment market is largely inoperative because lack of income among residents equates with a lack of demand for the usual housing accommodations. A land re-use program encompasses not only an organized rehabilitation effort on an expansive scale, but also a re-design, a rethinking of needed new concepts, and new philosophies of what the city and its neighborhoods should be and what functions it and they should serve.

(4) *New technology*

Effective slum clearance and low-cost housing techniques will come *if* inhibiting rules of the economic game are cleared away.

Development of a viable business market for housing construction technology to make slum clearance pay is crucial to the private enterprising system. The housing industry has frequently been criticized for technological backwardness. We can rehouse urban America only if the most advanced production technologies known are used and combined with flexible community planning which encompasses the single house, the multiple units, and the high-rise apartments into an integrated and aesthetic total community design. In this re-use of urban land, a direct and creative attack is necessary to reduce housing costs. There is no engineering or technological reason why entire bathroom units, kitchen units, and even apartment unit shells for high rise construction should not be mass produced and merely installed at the site. Monotony or drabness need not detract from mass rehabilitation on a neighborhood basis. Mass-produced modular units, pre-cutting, pre-fabrication can be turned out in different colors and textures and put together in a great many different ways to create a pleasing variety of models and designs. Careful site planning can assure privacy and individual variation. Recent years have seen many improvements in building materials (where firm bigness is the rule), but few in building and production techniques (where thousands of small builders and real estate speculators play the residential housing game). In the restructuring market flux tending toward organizational bigness, we can expect a measured response to induced market signals by corporate professional managers. As one business executive said to the author, "Currently we are excited about a housing plan done by a young architect in Florida. He has built one central module for $825 and thinks he can add two bedroom additions for about $500 each, and adding costs he did not have like a septic tank, he thinks we can build a very attractive four bedroom house for $3,500. We plan to do this soon on a pilot project. Incidentally, he and a VISTA worker built the central core of the house in 14 days—and may indicate ideas worth transferring to builders since money is labor."

(5) Skilled labor shortages

During periods of high levels of employment "bottlenecks" tend to appear, particularly in the construction, machine tool, and capital-investment industries. Among the bottlenecks in construction is the shortage of skilled union journeymen. In his testimony on the Housing and Urban Development Act of 1968, Burrell takes a polar position: "In spite of the talk about skilled building trades, the overwhelming majority of building tradesmen are high school drop-outs or less. A considerable number of them are scarcely literate. The day of the old line master carpenter, for example, is long gone and not particularly regretted. Today, housing is constructed by a dwindling army of semi-literate 'nail to the line' workers who can barely read a rule. A man who lays rafters does that and no more; a man who cuts out walls does that and no more; a man who nails joists or studs or raises walls performs that one simple function and no other. Indeed, there are sub-contractors in the building business who do nothing but nail down sub-flooring or roof sheathing.

"It is not necessary for any healthy man with a desire to earn his own way to spend six years as an apprentice carpenter. In fact, our builders tell us that if a man can't make it in six months, he never will. The artificial barriers set up by unions to control the construction labor supply under the guise of apprenticeship standards are an archaic luxury that this nation can no longer afford." (Berkeley G. Burrell, President, National Business League, Testimony on the Housing and Urban Development Act of 1968, Subcommittee on Housing and Urban Affairs, U. S. Senate Committee on Banking and Currency, March 22, 1968.)

Notwithstanding the power of skilled trade unions the ecological processes of change stemming from technology in method, materials, and processes seem inevitably to be changing the rules of the game. The construction industry, as one of the biggest single economic activity systems, remains labor intensive. Building and construction activities, on site, require less formal education for direct laborers than do most other labor intensive industries. Accordingly, construction activities can absorb substantial numbers of unemployed and currently underemployed urbanites. The urgency of housing the urban population presages a staunch refusal of leaders and public opinion to allow artificially created barriers, accruing benefits to a small group at the expense of the community, to delay "getting on with the job." As the market structure and technology change so do the rules governing play of the real estate game.

(6) *Money*

To minimize inflationary pressures, investment for economic growth must represent real savings, i.e., production minus consumption. In contrast to business investment, mortgage funds depend almost wholly upon individual savings. Personal saving, as we know, is a function of the levels of gross national income.

In 1960 with disposable personal income at $350.0 billion, personal savings amounted to $17.0 billion. In 1967 disposable personal income hit $544.6 billion; personal saving at this level of income was $38.7 billion for an absolute dollar gain of $21.7 billion representing more than a doubling of dollar savings between the two years. At the same time, the number of non-farm residential units constructed moved from 1,252,100 in 1960 to only 1,268,400 in 1967. Value of construction, in current dollars, increased only from $21.7 billion to $23.6 billion.

To emphasize relationships between the sectors it is noted that businessmen in 1960 retained $56.8 billion of corporate earnings while investing $74.8 billion, thus absorbing some $18 billion of personal savings; in 1967 retained business earnings amounted to $90.4 billion, gross private domestic investment hit $112.1 billion and business absorbed $21.7 billions of personal savings. Also significant in the disposition of real savings for the construction by state and local governments from the $12.2 billion rate in 1960 to $21.7 billion in 1967. As measured fund flows, business and local governments have been keen competitors for savings in this decade. Mortgage debt, however, that stood at $174.5 billion in 1960 rose dramatically over the entire seven year period to $294.0 billion, a 68 percent rise. The trend toward home ownership in suburbia continued unabated, but density of population within "inner cities" of the central urban places rose more rapidly than residential facilities; overcrowding accelerated the slum spread and urban environmental deterioration.

There seems little doubt that the federal government will continue to manipulate the home building, financial sector of the economy. The extent of activities will depend upon a value judgment of the degree to which the private housing market meets politically defined housing needs. Government interest in housing finance has shifted sharply in the post-war period. The financing market structure created by FHA and VA reduced downpayments, increased the length of the loan period, and lowered buyer qualification standards. Subsequent experience has demonstrated that long-term, easier mortgage provisions are sound lending practice. Through the years, however, FHA and VA government mortgage support programs have suburbanized America by servicing middle and upper income groups. As a result the private housing market has also serviced these same groups as their demands were reflected in the market place. In the financial institutional structure of the money market rests the means by which demands for low-cost housing can be reflected in the private housing market. In institutional market organization and land re-use lie the means to satisfy these market demands for urban low-cost housing.

Vesting a Housing Market Structure

The market for housing and neighborhood maintenance can function to halt slum spread. The slum rehabilitation process encompasses new land-use design, a revised pattern of residential arrangements along with commercial, industrial, educational, and recreational activities. Crucial to this housing market maintenance and/or development is to provide those conditions that entice middle income families with children to live in the neighborhood. Leadership will come not from economic passivists living in the slums but from economic and political activists. It is the middle income families enmeshed in the enterprising, freedom oriented American value system who become involved in the educational system's excellence, in recreational needs and facilities, and in adequate city services. To begin with, in the initial stages of developing a core city housing market, the type of housing offered, so long as it is decent, comfortable, and convenient, is secondary to establishment of a viable neighborhood environment. City services and excellence in schools, in parks and recreation facilities, in street maintenance, in transportation facilities, in police and fire protection, and in related basic utilities including some aesthetic charm provide the spark. Indigenous neighborhood leadership, esprit de corps, and pride in being a citizen in the neighborhood provide the momentum toward total environmental excellence.

Market functioning is a means to this environmental goal. Activist economic and social policies in the neighborhood or community must be compatible with the value system residents in the community wish to establish and maintain. Left to their own functioning, the signals in the real estate market fostering short-run profit-making frequently run counter to the neighborhood resident's value structure. The realtor's search for profits is not necessarily immoral but oftentimes his tactics (blockbusting, for example) are completely incompatible with the established residential neighborhood value system. The result is seen in the suburban exodus. Such private enterprising practices can be minimized only by a change in the rules governing the real estate game. Trade association ethical practice restraints are helpful.

Urban governmental ordinance controls with teeth can also assist in doing the job.

Financial institutions, supported by federal mortgages guarantees on core city residential properties in middle income neighborhoods, can reap competitive investment returns from middle income mortgage loans. City services and concerned middle class activist leadership can be depended upon to protect neighborhood integrity and property values. If the housing market, as reflected by private demands and public determined capital and service needs, can be made to work so as to provide those ingredients essential to the value system middle income families demand of their residential environment, the central city can clothe itself once again with activist, responsible, and interested leadership.

In the interest of urban environmental excellence, the market needs social-directed adjustment when the economic signals called are not in the community interest. The making of slums in the last decades has provided the enterprising system the means of optimizing short-term profit returns. Say's law "that supply creates its own demand" has been discredited by economists in advanced, monetized economies. Yet, the very fact that low-cost slum housing was available in the last decades assured occupancy concomitantly with the massive trek to the cities. The supply of low-cost living space, no matter how abject or rat infested, has created its own demand just through its availability. As slums spread and the supply increased, rising demand maintained high occupancy rates. Enterprising men, responding to profit-making signals, contributed readily to slum spread. With little or no thought of the impact on the total urban environment, and with manifest unconcern, short-term profit taking by absentee landlords has been termed "the name of the game." While governments have spent much time and billions of dollars on physical and human renewal in the urban place to stem the spread and renew the environment and resources of the slum wasteland, very little has been done to modify market functioning to make it less profitable to create and operate slum housing. Building inspection has been lax. Evasion of building codes, particularly by substantial owners of slum housing, has been standard operating procedure. Zoning restrictions have been stretched with the elasticity of rubber bands. The *Chicago Daily News*, March 23, 1968, reports confirmation of a quite typical market abuse to neighborhood environments and value standards. Lakeview, a desirable residential family neighborhood is embroiled in an angry fight over "four-plus-one" apartment buildings in the area. "These are shoddily constructed, five-story apartment houses designed to bring their owners a fat, fast buck, according to a study made by the Park West Community Association. . . ."

"These could be the slums of tomorrow," said Alderman Thomas Rosenberg, a legislator not known for wild views.

The News noted that the buildings contain 60 studio and one-bedroom units on a 75 foot lot and that the builder need put up only $10,000 or $20,000 of his money to create the $300,000 or $400,000 structure, so generous is the mortgage financing.

The residents, self-organized into the Park West Association, commissioned an architect to make a study of the four-plus-one construction and to encourage new construction more in keeping with the desires and value system of the neighborhood residents. As reported by the News, the architect observed "these structures have replaced older and lower density structures with higher density structures, containing efficiency and one bedroom apartments. Families with children are precluded from living in these structures because of the small apartment size."

Therein lies the key, reports the News. "The four-plus-ones (so named because they consist of four floors of apartments set over an English basement) are not illegal under the city's building code, nor are they in conflict with the existing zoning classifications in the area where they are being built. They are undesirable from the point of view of the community now represented in the area."

The real issue in this instance is the dichotomy existing between the rules governing the business game in the real estate market and the system of values held by the family oriented residential home owners in the neighborhood.

Economic events and behavior are subject to guidance and direction by tax financial aid, and functional service policies at the federal, state, and local levels of government. Federal tax policy provides no deterrent to discourage slum creation through making such activities less profitable. To the contrary, the reference above "so generous is the mortgage financing," reflects federal policy and federal agency "eagerness" to add to the supply of housing any and all kinds of multiple unit housing to ease urbanizing housing pressures. Federal tax policy which allows the same structure to be depreciated over and over again each time commercial investment properties change ownership discourages incentives to improve and upgrade slum housing. Such housing is depreciated quickly and cash flows are augmented if improvement expenditures are not committed. Federal tax policy that specified investment credit allowance both for new individual family residential construction and housing refurbishment (town houses for example) would provide strong inducement for neighborhood improvement. Federal policies, such as FHA, and VA, designed to positively assist home-ownership among low income earners and thus reduce absentee slum landlordism in the core city would tend to augment neighborhood esprit de corps and participation in community affairs. The federal rent supplement and turn-key programs are measures attempting to work through the private housing market to upgrade available accommodations and to increase housing supply through shifting the demand curve for low-cost housing ownership up and to the right. To allow deductions for neighborhood assessments incurred for improvement projects and to individuals for residential property improvement much as local taxes paid are deductible from federal tax obligations would also provide incentive for structural upgrading in residential neighborhoods.

At the local level of government direct policy actions are indicated. Enforce building codes; judiciously plan and design zoning requirements in line with zonal area functions. Appraisal and assessments practices should be designed to recognize fully the inflated land values in the core city. In perennial frustration, city planners and urban economic developers state that this or that development is not feasible in model city slum neighborhoods BECAUSE OF THE HIGH PRICE OF LAND. If this is true, and it is, then the property assessment and the taxes levied on the land should be the central tax base consideration and not the old, dilapidated, rat infested structure which is incongruously referred to as a residence. As another approach, slum residential units not lived in by the owner could be taxed as commercial, business property since it is in effect held for business investment purposes. A gross receipt tax on rents collected would also tend to make slum landlordism less profitable.

On the positive side purposive actions can make low-cost housing and middle income neighborhoods attractive for family living and as a business investment. The means lie in broad-based programs to upgrade publicly provided neighborhood services, efficient and accessible transportation modes adequate to meet neighborhood mobility needs, and a leadership in the neighborhood to monitor and encourage do-it-yourself programs designed to revitalize and upgrade living conditions for families in the core city neighborhood.

On the private sector side of the housing market ledger, businessmen can revitalize their city and their markets by:

1. providing needed neighborhood leadership through encouraging employees to get involved.

2. forming voluntary business associations, through local chambers of commerce for example, to actively work in urban economic development projects. These might include: (a) formation of a private revolving fund to provide a financial base; (b) to purchase and improve reclaimable slum properties; (c) to build new houses and finance their purchase by middle or low income buyers who otherwise could not afford home-ownership; (d) to assist in the provision of day care centers in low and middle income neighborhoods staffed by volunteers; (e) to try through schools, churches, business groups, and local governments to improve neighborhood recreation facilities.

As the view of the city and its environs is brought into focus the inescapable need for political supervision over economic activities and privately generated externalities becomes evident. However, the game is pluralism at its best. If our cities are to survive, if urban living it to be the center of economic, social, political, and cultural activity, ALL institutions and individuals will need to work individually and together toward the mutual goal of excellence in all phases of urban life. If the city is best defined as a highly monetized market environment, then, each sub-market must remain dynamic and responsive to environmental requirements. Each sub-market, in turn, must call the right signals if free enterprise is to remain viable and do the job that needs doing in urban centers.

.. 12 ..

Economic Baselines in Urban Development

URBAN problems today require sweeping changes in our economic thinking and approaches to urban economic development. We cannot ignore the massive population growth nor the shift of the population to the urban place. We cannot ignore the accelerating demands of a clamoring urban population for jobs, housing, better education facilities and programs, for manpower retraining and human rehabilitation, for improved public health facilities, and other improvements. Certainly we cannot ignore the new role of government in the urban place and the partnership developing between the public and private sectors. We have seen that interacting technological changes can cause violent chain reactions, which perhaps while advancing man's economic and social interests in the longer run may have a deleterious short run impact upon employment, income, and the economic health of the urban place. Change which occurs too fast disturbs living styles and work patterns, may precipitate social upheavals, and influences significantly the quality of human life in the urban political economy.

There is urgent need to cure existing urban political economy system malfunctionings, and the time for adaptation and adjustment is short. Technological physical innovations have catapulted the American society into an intensified urbanized environment which is spawning critically serious social and cultural conflicts. Kenneth Baulding, University of Michigan economist, has said in this regard "a failure to advance in the physical and biological sciences for the next 25 years would not present mankind with any serious problems but the failure to advance in the world of the social sciences would be fatal. We need Social Inventions to correct

146

some of our problems." (Baulding, *Impact of the Social Sciences,* 1966.)

THE MARKET REVISITED

In its simplest construct the market is people. As we have observed, market behavior extracts incentives and fosters human motivations. In a democratic political economy markets are not established; markets develop.

People engaged in the exchange of goods and services for other goods and services constitute the market process. Market behavior is institutionalized and people are wont to behave in the same pattern as do their peers. However, in the emerging urban environment changing technology altered the conditions of market supply. Lassez-faire capitalism evolved into oligopolistic capitalism. Technology also variegated supply on such a scale as to make the choice selection of one variation over another a frustration of individual freedom of choice. Give a child a choice of a vanilla or a chocolate ice cream cone and he will quickly and freely make his choice, but take him into an ice cream parlor with 35 distinct and beautiful flavors, all advertised in color pictures on the wall, and you now have a frustrated individual, trapped by his environment, hardly able to exercise a free choice. This is more often than not the prevailing feeling in the urban marketplace.

Moreover, in altering the conditions of supply and the structure of economic organization, the large corporation and the conglomerate firm made the intervention of the state a necessary directing force of much economic activity in the interest of economic order and stability. Fiscal and monetary policy are invoked to sustain aggregate demand and investment flows to spur an ever growing industrial capacity to produce more goods and services to satisfy an augmented demand. In addition, the several levels of government collaborate to administer variegated welfare-state type programs ranging from medicare to hospital construction to unemployment compensation to man-power retraining to aid to dependent children to urban renewal. The issue that stands out is that the roles played in the political economy at all levels of government constitute a stance, not a doctrine; an attitude, not a coherent set of theoretical dogmas; and finally a leadership style without much substance. Certainly in the emerging world of measured economics we in the economics profession have learned the how of many things. The discipline of economics is appreciably more scientific today than it was in the time of

Mill or Marshall, or even Keynes. But if economics is to be more than a mere collection of tools and techniques its body of knowledge must continue to inspire men to struggle for themselves and their fellowmen. Deep in the American creed lie fundamental beliefs in justice and fair-play; alongside are the credos that are inherent in the American socio-political-economic system: order, logic, and purpose. These are hallmarks of physical technology and its innovation and they apply with equal force in the moral realm of our viable democratic system. American democracy in its urban setting is individualist, optimistic, and rational.

Technologically we are reaching a point where we can do almost anything we want; certainly we have the technological means and the engineering know-how to solve urban physical problems. The major problem is "system" and the reaching of a consensus by American society as to what it wants to do with the skills and knowledges we are acquiring. Through its existing institutional structure, the American society can communicate to those who direct our affairs the need to restore, preserve, and promote an abstraction. In this case the abstraction about which we need to educate the democracy is the *Market* as a behavioral system that will advance man's economic and social status in our changing urban world.

University of Chicago economist, Milton Friedman, argues well the advantages of the market as an institutional arrangement. He deplores the tendency, in this country and throughout the world, to use political rather than market mechanisms to solve social and individual problems. He states:

> The tendency to turn to the government for solutions promotes violence in at least three ways:
> 1. It exacerbates discontent.
> 2. It directs discontent at persons, not circumstances.
> 3. It concentrates great power in the hands of identifiable individuals.
>
> 1. The political mechanism enforces conformity. If 51 percent vote for more highways, all 100 percent will have to pay for them. If 51 percent vote against highways, all 100 percent must go without them.
> Contrast this with the market mechanism. If 25 percent want to buy cars, they can, each at his own expense. The other 75 percent neither get nor pay for them. Where the products are separable, the market system enables each person to get what he votes for. There can be unanimity without conformity. No one has to submit. . . .

2. If a law, or action by a public official, is all that is needed to solve a problem, then the *people* who refuse to vote for the law, or who fail to act, are responsible for the problem. . . .

Circumstances—the fact that resources are limited—make it impossible to meet all demands. But to each citizen it will appear—often correctly—that he is being frustrated by his fellow men, not by nature. Men have always reached beyond their grasp—but they have not always attributed failure to the selfishness of their fellow men. . . .

3. Political power is not only more visible but far more concentrated than market power can ever be. . . .

A free and orderly society is a complex structure. We understand but dimly its many sources of strength and weakness. The growing resort to political solutions is not the only and may not be the main source of the resort to violence that threatens the foundation of freedom. But it is one that we can do something about. We must husband the great reservoir of tolerance in our people, their willingness to abide by majority rule—not waste it trying to do by legal compulsion what we can do as well or better by voluntary means. (Milton Friedman, "Politics and Violence," *Newsweek*, June 24, 1968, p. 90.)

Within the parameters of the game predicated by the classical economists, in staunch opposition to the pre-conditions of mercantilism, was a strong reliance upon natural laws. In straightforward language, the rules of the game were:

a. promote individual freedom,

b. destroy power, privilege, and prerogative,

c. extoll and provide for individual incentive and initiative.

Given these, within severe structural parameters, Adam Smith's "Great Unseen Hand" (competition) would constitute a "system" which would at all times cause public and private interests to coincide.

Mr. Eugene Black, while still President of the World Bank, in 1961 spoke at the University of Georgia on economic development experiences of underdeveloped countries. One striking phenomenon was the inevitable poverty amidst slums which developed concurrently with and contiguous to the emerging industrial complex. The phenomenon was explained by Mr. Black as an economic and cultural lag typical of industrial development throughout history in free enterprise systems. It takes time for the institutional market structure of a monetized market economy to develop out of a semi-barter precondition; and it takes time for the increased productivity forthcoming from the industrial technology to percolate down to the workers, the buying public, through the producers' goods market for labor. So, in the meantime, slums and shanty towns emerge.

In the modern urban political economy, the market environment is already highly monetized. The necessary institutional arrangements are operating and extant. The task now facing society is not to innovate and create new institutions but rather to change certain rules of the economic game to restore to the market its guiding and controlling function. Through various means, including subsidy incentives to the producer and to the householder, the market can be made to guide production and consumption. The credit ratings of low income individuals can be bolstered by government guarantees of private loans and by subsidies to borrowers to sustain market demand. Investment flows will continue to reflect the demands of the people in both the public and private sectors. And if properly conceived and programmed, the rules of the game governing market control of economic activities would eliminate large segments of unsatisfied demand, such as urban low cost housing. Properly designed rules of the game would remain flexible, provide a viable market functioning to meet all basic needs of the urban population, maintain free enterprise incentive, sustain individual freedom of choice, and enhance human dignity. Keynes showed conclusively that the whole free enterprise market system was indeterminant. By proclaiming that the market should serve man rather than man serve the market, society can design the market to serve its needs. The highly monetized nature of market functioning provides a key for market design, for "exchange" in the marketplace is a function of income and, in turn, creates income.

MARKET DESIGN

Aesop said "Beware lest you lose the substance by grasping at the shadow." Harry R. Hall, President of Michigan State Chamber of Commerce, puts it this way: "Now no longer is it enough to modernize, to catch up with the present because the present doesn't live here any more. We have to try to lead the present so that at some precise point in the future we and the then future will arrive together. We have to futurize. Now, if man achieves new stabilities, they must be of a different kind, ones based on dynamics not on statics; ones he invents and maintains, not ones he has inherited and can take for granted." ("Leadership Demands in a Demanding Society," a speech presented at the University of Georgia, June 17, 1968.)

If restructuring and revitalizing the market function by rewriting rules of the economic game and hence modifying behavior can be postulated as a means of attacking urban problems, there has to be a conceptual understanding of the economic system as a whole. There must be ways and means to formulate system goals, to allow the price mechanism to allocate and guide the utilization of resources, and to achieve for society those advantages accruing to specialization in the division of labor and capital.

In a highly monetized urban political economy, the system exchange processes in the basic market functioning. Consumption expenditure flows, plus investment expenditure flows, plus government expenditure flows equals gross national income. Economically, this is the best measure we have to aggregate material well-being. Market rules of the game necessarily must sustain and augment economic and concomitant monetary flows.

The Household

a. As a social and economic unit in society, each of us as individuals, as members of families, and as members of other social groups must find stability within ourselves. Autonomy of the individual underlies integrity, character development, and improvement of living styles in urban places.

b. Householders need to seek out and pursue that course which involves them in community affairs. Men are what they think and do, hence their work, their church, their social and community activities are essential aspects of successful life styles in a healthy urban environment. An essential prerogative of a demanding urban society is institutional provision for continuing education, not just vocational training, not just more specialized understanding in the humanities. Looking ahead, urban populations will need continuing education that:

(1) enables householders to comprehend the meaning, the values, the relevancy of the flood of information cascading upon them at an accelerating pace from all directions in this computerizing age;

(2) allows understanding by householders of the relationships between sustainable facts and ideas and between one idea versus another idea:

(3) enables householders to grasp full understanding of new concepts and relationships as institutional and behavioral patterns are redesigned to foster ecological adjustment to new environmental conditions;

(4) grants householders the capacity to exercise ethical value judgments on changing institutional concepts, changing environmental needs, and their relevance to the whole autonomous urban community complex.

The Consumers Goods Market

a. Demand and supply relationships are seldom at rest. The continuing processes of reaction indicate the changes, large or small, occuring in each. If demand rises it is signaled by higher product prices which leads in turn to an increasing supply response and larger quantities sold, perhaps new firms to handle the products, and continuous adjustment. Demand and supply adjustments really never stop, never rest, as they constantly are adjusting to each other in the multitudes of product markets in the urban place. An initial rule might be: do not get excited about piecemeal spasmodic shortages or surpluses. Demand and supply adjustments occur through time, so give the system the time it needs.

b. In the monetized consumer goods market, the level of activity is determined at that point where the marginal buyer meets the marginal seller. So long as the buyer is free to choose his item of purchase and the seller is free to sell to any buyer who is willing to meet or better his reservation price, the market price mechanism rations the goods and services exchanged among buyers according to their tastes and income abilities to buy. With the freedom to choose goes the equality of rights among individuals in the marketplace. Rule: Let equality of prices to all buyers alike prevail. Ability and willingness to pay the price becomes the single criterion governing the market exchange process.

c. The economic condition of individual freedom is the "right" to participate in market exchange processes. If this "right" is a dependent function of income, then society must act to provide that income through employment or otherwise. The exchange of goods and services for goods and services is a sort of positive-sum game in which both parties benefit. We sometimes forget that consumption performs an essential economic function as well as an economic expression of freedom of action and choice.

d. In a highly monetized market, income and its distribution is the key to economic viability. The urban political economy system needs to recruit the full measure of economic leadership from the private and the public sectors to sustain growing income levels and to maintain expanding economic flows through the market. Firms providing goods or services respond with alacrity to their demanding customers. Rule: The profit incentive provides strong motivation in the urban based service-oriented political economy. If, as the post-war period has shown, a high rate of growth and income can be sustained by a high rate of technological innovation, then it makes economic sense to subsidize new technology as a means of developing a continuing spate of new growth industries.

THE PUBLIC SERVICE SECTOR

a. No set of dogma or philosophical bent provides a ready answer to differentiate those services that are best supplied by the urban based government and services that are best supplied to customers by the private enterprising sector. In either case the householder pays, but in the private market freely and without coercion. As a general rule of thumb, even though circumstances and traditional practices differ widely between urban places, it seems that wherever private use of a product can be measured and priced, it is legitimately considered a private market item. When such is not the case as with streets, fire and police protection, public health, ad infinitum, the product or service is a proper and legitimate function of the public sector.

b. Public services designed to serve all citizens alike and equally necessarily require the exercise of some control. The rationing function of the price mechanism, according to income and ability and willingness to pay the market determined price, controls the use of privately provided goods and services. Because payment is indirect for public goods and services, more overt controls are exerted. In regard to the overcrowding of streets by harried individuals going to and from work downtown, the demand for street use outruns the supply and slows usage to a mere crawl during rush hours. Result: a harried driver, a harried traffic officer, a slow moving vehicle, and a long line waiting at each traffic light. This is a typical condition of scarcity; and scarcity, whether for road space, food, clothing, or automobiles always makes social controls essential. Despite all the inconvenience, when traffic pressures exceed the normal workable capacity of city thoroughfares, drivers are surprisingly polite and fair to each other in giving the other fellow a break on facilities intended to satisfy individual demands more or less equally.

Rule: Public entities can plan and set priorities in providing public services. Within the foreseeable future, however, scarcity conditions are inevitable. Controls will be necessary as a matter of extending freedom under conditions of scarcity to effect the orderly and equal distribution of these scarce publically provided resources outside the monetized market process.

THE INVESTMENT MARKET

If we may reason from the general to the particular, demand for goods and services is a function of income; income is a function of employment; employment, in turn, is a function of investment; and, to round out our model flows, investment is a function of the level of demand. Induced investment flows are a reaction to market signals indicating a change in demand and supply relationships. Autonomous investment flows reflect implementation of technological innovation typically designed for new products or product quality improvement or cost reduction.

a. Employment as a function of investment is no longer only an individual, firm, or industry concern. Mass unemployment is a matter of public concern, and governments at all levels, particularly the urban metropolitan governments, must face the problem directly with the assistance of the federal government. The economic condition of freedom requires the right allocation of resources and the creation of adequate employment opportunities so that the abundance of goods and services created contribute to an improvement of living and working life styles in urban places. *Rule*: Investment expenditure flows are the joint concern of the private and public sectors as a function that is vital to attaining economic health in the urban community. Joseph Monsen states: "If all the effects are taken into account, the government is undoubtedly the main factor in determining the direction in the use of our resources." (R. Joseph Monsen, Jr., *Modern American Capitalism*, 1963, p. 52.)

b. Enterprising managers, in large and in small firms, are problem solvers entrusted with the responsibility of satisfying market demands. They are in essence "practicing" economists. In the post-war period we have seen emerging out of economic doctrines what is variously referred to as "management science," "operations research," "linear programming," and "decision theory." This is a body of theory involving information compilation, processing, and interpretation techniques which have been established as an independent managerial decision-making tool. Max Ways in the January, 1967, issue of *Fortune* says "system management involves ways of arranging ends and means so that decision-makers have clearer ideas of the choices open to them and better ways of measuring both expectations and objectives." Investment decisions are subject to more rational analysis, and the marginal efficiency of capital can be determined with considerable assurance. Guesswork and hunches are no longer appropriate or adequate. Utilization of systems management techniques in determining the kinds and levels of investment flows to sustain urban place development will be a step forward. This new innovative discipline applied to the broad social, economic, and political problems of the urban place should enable us to do a much more acceptable job in appraising community needs, setting priorities, and in effectively meeting environmental production, employment, and income requirements. Rule: Coordinated public-private planning can project employment requirements and estimate investment levels by kind and amount to maintain an economically healthy balance between job opportunities and job seekers. However, society should be fully cognizant of the dangers of vesting unbalanced power in the evolving corporate-urban technocracy. The 1966 Report of the President's Commission on Technology, Automation, and Economic Progress, *Technology and the American Economy*, extolls the virtues of corporate excellence: "Just as the concentration of research efforts produced such radically new inventions as intercontinental ballistic missiles and Polaris submarines, concentrations of similar scale on more difficult economic and social problems could contribute to meeting our human and social needs if the political consensus could be implemented." The large firms of the corporate-military complex described by President Eisenhower are increasingly involved in implementing new urban technologies. The public sector must guard against any unbalanced concentration of power in any industrial coalition addicted to public subsidized research and development and guaranteed risk-free profits. Where public monies and the public interest are involved, a general but impeccable public supervision of firm price-output policies and behavior is a cardinal rule of the enterprising market game. (Essential reading in this regard is Richard Austin Smith's *Corporations in Crisis*, the drama of management under stress. Particularly see "General Electric: A Case of Antitrust," pp. 113-166. About this book Peter Drucker says "This is above all a book about people, their strengths and their weaknesses, their visions and their cowardices. It therefore succeeds where most

business executives fall down so conspicuously; it gets across
that business enterprise is a human achievement").

c. Investment flows originate in savings and bank credit.
Personal savings accrue when individuals do not spend their total
income, i.e., that part not spent is saved. Corporations also save
as undistributed profits are accumulated. Bank credit is used
most commonly for self-liquidating short-term business investments such as inventory. The relative proportions in private investments flows are about as follows: corporate savings, 60%;
personal savings, 20%; bank credit, 20%. Society needs to understand that existing pricing-output policies of the large private
corporations and conglomerates puts these firms in the role of
social trusteeship. Society's savings are largely governed by the
Fortune 500 corporations, and their investment decisions tend to
determine the direction of economic advance, the level of investment flows, the job opportunities created by number and
kind, and in addition govern the pace of change. Supplementing
the large corporation are the trust departments of a dominant few
large banks, insurance companies, mutual funds, and private
pension funds. However, these institutions tend to supplement
rather than enter into decisions calling the basic direction and
kind and level of technological implementations attained by the
flow of investment funds.

Since 1961, at the federal level, the emphasis on instability has
been replaced by a more progressive growth philosophy as investment flows were conditioned.

There have been:

a. reductions in corporate taxes to stimulate investment flows
and increases in corporate taxes to discourage investment flows
as an attempt to dampen inflationary pressures;

b. reductions in personal income taxes to stimulate spending
and saving and increases likewise to dampen consumer exuberance
and inflationary pressures;

c. alternating tight and easy money policies exercised by the
Federal Reserve System to purposively adjust the cost of money
so as to encourage or discourage investment flows as environmental conditions signaled;

d. a change in depreciation allowance schedules and investment credits on tax liabilities to both encourage and discourage
investment flows;

e. a multitude of government efforts to speed or retard
or redirect investment flows through such programs as the war

on poverty, model cities, urban renewal, low-cost public housing, the inter-state highway system, and areo-space and basic research in the billions of dollars providing a spur to private investment flows and add to this, of course, expenditures at the local level of government. Expenditures increasing at ten percent per year to put the necessary social capital overhead in place to support a growing urban population are nonetheless still deficient. Also urban governments build the capital base on which the private enterprising sector has expanded and which it demands the public sector do.

Rule: Saving at one point flows into investment at some other point in the economy to maintain viability, capacity and productivity, and to create jobs. Maximum purchasing power is best considered as the volume and distribution of real income in the urban political economy which correlates private and public spending. A consumption and investment pattern consistent with the urban environmental condition for balanced growth of the public and private sectors would benefit the urban entity as an autonomous whole. Essential conditions to achieve balanced urban development are:

a. that investment flows be programmed and balanced in the urban environment in regards to private and public facility expansion;

b. that income distribution between public and private consumption, savings, and investment flows be consistent with those urban priorities which depend upon publicly provided services and capital facilities;

c. that the distribution of both private and public services and facilities be consistent with determined environmental consumption requirements in the complex, urbanized economy. Collective consumption needs are the legitimate concerns of the enterprising businessmen responding to market signals.

THE MARKET FOR PRODUCER'S GOODS AND SERVICES

Exchange processes in this market create and distribute income. Levels of economic flows in both the consumer goods market and the investment goods market reflect the generation and distribution of income in the market for producer goods and services. This is the market in which the actual allocation and utilization of resources are reflected in exchange processes, encompassing the basic ingredients of economic growth. This is the market that has been most prone to weakness, to strife among

participants, to economic resource waste, and has exhibited those
malfunctions such as mass unemployment, disadvantageous social
externalities, and economic instabilities that have led us into a
neo-mercantilistic mixed economy.

A. The Employment Act of 1946 requires that this nation
work toward maximum use of its productive capacity, including
a full utilization of manpower and brainpower, physical technology, and natural resources.

Rule 1: In the market for producer goods and services, public
and private policies should be coordinated to assure steady optimum economic growth in real terms in accordance with balanced
urban environmental requirements. This postulates the setting of
a priority of national goals, which is clearly within the intent and
philosophy of the Employment Act of 1946.

Rule 2: Coordinated policy should apportion the allocation
of resources, natural and human, in accordance with relative
priorities of public-private sector needs in urban centers.

Rule 3: Social policy should combine economic progress,
through the allocation and utilization of resources in the production process and the distribution of the abundance created, with
economic justice, the protection of individual rights, and the
preservation of human dignity.

B. Demand and supply interactions and continuing adjustments tempered greatly by technological innovations provide
an effective price mechanism in the producer goods market for
natural and capital goods resources, their allocation and use.

Rule: Maintain public supervision over the private concentrations of natural and capital resource ownership and control to
minimize socially adverse monopolistic practices. Restructure the
federal, state, and local tax laws, tax bases, and tax administration so as to achieve equity between householder interests as
consumers and organized producers. (See the eighteen-year record
of Paul H. Douglas, Senator from Illinois, for guidance and rules.)

C. Neo-mercantilism, the mixed economy, was invoked by
society to solve the system malfunctioning leading to massive
unemployment. People, even in the strictest economic sense, are
the source of economic problems and the key to economic success. Again keep in mind that throughout our discourse the
definition of "system" always connotes behavior in one sense
or another.

In the exchange processes of the labor market lie fundamental
issues of urban environmental development. Income, as we have

noted, is key to the level of economic activity in the consumer and investment goods markets. Because wages and salaries constitute some 70 to 75 percent of all householder income the decision to work combined with the opportunity to work is molding urban economic and political policies as an important environmental conditioner. There is nothing intrinsic in human nature which assures that all the tasks necessary to support a very interdependent, specialized, technologically-oriented urban society will be performed. Rather, the psychological human make-up provides a potential which when properly conditioned, educated, and motivated can be enticed through outside incentives to perform in one way or another. The key, at this point, is training, education, and motivation.

We have noted that political rights are hollow without concomitant economic rights. Economic rights, in turn, are meaningless unless concomitant obligations are accepted and fulfilled. In the long run, economic advance depends upon productivity improvements. This, in turn, is a function of human motivation to work, to learn, to develop one's potential, creativity, and drive. An urban society can hardly hope to preserve economic freedom from want, deprivation, and slums unless it can look forward to an advancing level of productivity and output in both the public and private sectors. The public sector can provide the facilities and opportunities for education and training. The private sector can provide the organized research and employment opportunities backed up by public sector policies as necessary. Personal motivation is a more ethical concept, a cultural condition, and subject to external incentives. The market is fully capable, if designed to function equitably and freely to grant equality of opportunity to all individuals, of motivating individuals with cogency and vigor. Man does not live by bread alone, and the market responds to fulfill a myriad of aspirations.

Confusion about positive incentives is always present. It is true that there are thousands among the hard core unemployed who prefer handouts to work. It is also true that these individuals have been alienated, unwanted, non-involved, and are unable to participate in the economic or political life of the community. It is not surprising that they lack psychological motivation. Looking to the future, urban society needs to combine political freedom and involvement with economic freedom and involvement.

Rule: Coordinated private-public sector actions to vitalize democratic processes involving all citizens and a combined effort to prepare people for participation in urban labor markets and to assure each a job opportunity commensurate with his qualifications will tend to involve people in economic processes. A dynamic market can provide the motivation and the means of distributing abundance to those involved equitably and freely. Involvement in work activity, the decision to work, will probably more than any other single factor determine future life styles in the urban complex. The crisis of our cities must be met with the creation of real democracy—political, social, and economic.

In summary, society is saying through its enacted legislative philosophy since the 1930's that:

1. every American is entitled (has a right) to a minimum standard of housing, of nutrition, of education, of medical care, a minimum American standard of living;

2. earnings not welfare should be the primary source of income for those able to work.

This general philosophy is familiar and seems to be universally held and accepted in public policy. This means, then, that:

1. society has an obligation to assure a decent minimal standard of living for each of its members in its own self-interest and integrity as an autonomous body politic;

2. society, through its political economy system, has an obligation to provide useful and productive work opportunities for all members of society within their capacity to perform;

3. society has the obligation and the authority to motivate (and direct) men as necessary to see to it that necessary work is performed.

This is not to reinstate motivations of fear or hunger as legitimate social policy. Rather, it is an obligation to assure that a viable market emits vigorous signals that provide outside stimulants and incentives sufficiently strong to involve men in the work process. In hard-headed business terms, society is saying to each individual able to work: "Look friend, we stand ready to exchange goods and services for goods and services. When you give, you receive in equitable proportion." It will be a significant accomplishment to devise institutions providing for urban economic development and for democratic participation. We see a beginning in model cities and urban renewal. Perhaps, however, the real crux lies in the direction of vitalized democratic processes in urban government affairs and the increasingly inter-dependent partnership of the public and private sectors at the local level.

Rule: For those individuals unable to work and for those

individuals whose capacity is insufficient, though working, to earn sufficient minimal income, society should, in its own economic interest, assure an income distribution to sustain minimal living standards. Whether this policy be a family allowance plan or some version of the so-called negative income tax is immaterial to this discourse. In principle, the assurance of minimal income and living standards is a vital step along the way to economic freedom. That freedom that can come only through the exercise of free choice among alternatives to maximize one's utilities in a viable market-oriented economy of abundance. It seems unlikely within the structure of the American political economy that urban environmental requirements can be met with anything of an optimal rate of economic growth. In turn, it seems unlikely that we can attain optimal economic growth unless we revitalize market demands and market viability by maintaining an income distributive system which assures each individual a minimal standard of living, a freedom of choice in the market exchange process, and a feeling of involvement in economic flows and growth. Keep in mind that since passage of the Employment Act of 1946, during an era of increasing abundance, public policy has tended to reverse long standing traditional thought. Now consumption is pushed vigorously as a means of sustaining greater employment levels. More goods have to be produced so the economy can accomplish full employment, a fuller use of productive capacity and resource utilization. Somehow, the "produce so that you can consume" tradition has been reversed. Now we push for higher production as a means of keeping factories operating, stores open, trains moving, and people at work. Realistically, in view of the accelerating pace of scientific and technological change augmenting productivity and output, material policy is on a treadmill. Rationally, employment of men is economically desirable only if the goods and services are needed. In view of the environmental needs of urban places, the setting of production priorities should be obvious and easy. Providing minimal incomes to all to assure minimal standards of living is a starting point for producing goods that are needed. With income this augmented demand will signal in market processes and elicit prompt response. Consumption is an economic function and an essential prerequisite to the condition of economic freedom.

ALTERNATIVES IN URBAN DEVELOPMENT

There seems always to exist a considerable lag between the everchanging reality of man's environmental conditions and his rigid mold of ideology about how "things ought to be." In his book *Change and Habit*, Toynbee observes that America has a history of technological radicalism and social conservatism which cannot be combined. In urging a revitalized market orientation it is suggested that this is not the time for introspective analyses but for creative action. Further in the turbulence of our times leadership must not be merely moral exhortations alone, but in the American culture economic leadership must somehow bring with it a payment in cash. This the market can do. We need to restore, redesign, restructure, and legitimize the market institution as the guide, the control, and the center of economic freedom in the urban political economy.

Three distinct alternatives are offered to urban America at the present time: (1) sudden disaster through riot, devastation, and revolution (the city of today is an ideal setting for interminable guerilla warfare); (2) a slower stagnation and decay as cities seep deeper into the morass of slums, poverty, despair, and decay amidst a "do nothing" society until eventually the bottom falls out and society itself explodes; (3) an ecological adjustment to the economic, social, political, and cultural needs and conditions of our highly monetized, urbanized, industrialized, specialized environment. The one choice society does not have is to return to the simplistic "good old days" of an agricultural economy.

Michael Harrington's *The Other America* warned the nation of the hazards of neglecting the slum imprisoned poor. Yale University psychologist, Kenneth Kenniston in his *The Uncommitted* gave the nation a subtle and most perceptive analysis of alienated youth and spelled out reasons for youth's rebellion against adult standards. Jane Jacob, much discussed social critic, in her *The Death and Life of the Great Cities* excoriates the ruthless decivilization of human life styles in the big city.

If America is to meet the demands of its urban population and the needs of the urban environment, while lacking the preconditions necessary for realistic comparative analysis and judgment, its political and economic leadership must innovate, not just imitate; act creatively, not just react; program, not just protest; perform, not just proclaim; solve, not just resolve; accelerate, not just vacillate.

The urban political economy system needs to equate human development with urban economic development. The urban political economy system needs to encompass and coordinate those broad social, economic, and political issues of today and to-morrow that are interrelated, interacting, and interdependent. The major issues confronting the public or private sectors in the urban environment do not exist in isolation. They are as intricately interwoven as are the public and private sectors. As knowledge becomes more specialized, as urban society becomes more complex, all social problems become more interdependent. The urban-centered political economy system must provide a studied theoretical political economy framework and a sense of general direction for each major urban antonomous unit in the broader framework of the total national community—the total society.

Index